Truth Lies in Twilight
The Prophecy

By Elena Olympia Collins

Copyright © 2025 Elena Olympia Collins
ISBN 978-1-7638380-2-4

All rights reserved. No parts of this book may be reproduced in any form without prior written permission of the copyright owners. All images in this book have been reproduced with the knowledge and prior consent of the artists concerned, and no responsibility is accepted by author or publisher for any infringement of copyright or otherwise arising from the contents of this publication. Every effort has been made to ensure that credits accurately comply with information supplied. The author apologizes for any inaccuracies that may be present and will resolve inaccuracies or missing information in a subsequent reprinting of this book.
If you would like to contribute to the ongoing improvement of this book, or any of the author's other titles, you can send your suggestions for improvement to tarotwelldone@gmail.com. Please note that the account is not regularly monitored and a reply is not guaranteed. Impactful suggestions will receive named acknowledgement in a subsequent reprinting of this book.

Discover the Tarot as Never Seen Before

From the acclaimed author Elena Olympia Collins comes **Tarot Well Done** - a groundbreaking exploration that goes beyond intuition and into the structured language of the Rider-Waite tarot deck.

Praised for its depth, clarity, and originality, Collins demystifies tarot by revealing the symbolism, color theory, and numerical patterns that form the foundation of every reading. With close to 40 years of expertise, she challenges traditional approaches, encouraging readers to see tarot as a language rather than just a divination tool.

Described as thought-provoking and meticulously researched, **Tarot Well Done** offers a fresh perspective for both beginners and seasoned practitioners alike. It's a book that has reshaped the way readers interpret the cards - unlocking a structured, reliable, and deeply insightful approach to tarot reading.

Whether you're new to tarot or seeking a more profound understanding, this book will illuminate the path.

Join the journey. Challenge the narrative. **Read Tarot Well Done.**

Find **Tarot Well Done** at Barnes and Noble, Amazon, Walmart and all great booksellers. Available in Paperback, Hardback, Large-print, eBook and Audiobook. Soon to be released in Hindi.

Table of contents

PROLOGUE 7

INTRODUCTION 9

1 GENESIS 12
   THE PROPHECY 14
   THE LIFE CONTEXT 17

2 STAGECRAFT 19

3 THE MILLENNIUM PACT 22
   THE NEW AMERICAN PRESIDENT 22
   THE MAN WITH 5 LETTERS IN HIS NAME 23
   A REMARKABLE PRESIDENTIAL ELECTION CYCLE 31
   AN UNHOLY ALLIANCE 32
   THE SECOND THREAD 35
   THE 1972 PECULIARITY 44

4 ARCHITECTS OF CHAOS 46
   DISTRIBUTION OF POWER 46
   INSTITUTIONS AND NORMS 47
   IDEOLOGICAL AND CULTURAL VALUES 49
   ECONOMIC SYSTEMS AND GLOBAL INTERDEPENDENCE 50

5 THE CRADLES IGNITE 51
   HISTORICAL AND CULTURAL ROOTS 51
   GEO-POLITICAL IDENTITY 52
   POLITICAL AND ECONOMIC SYSTEMS 53
   CRACKS IN THE FOUNDATION 54
   FIFTH-GENERATIONAL WARFARE 58
   A SPARK IN SYRIA? 61

6 ONE MAN'S STAND 66
   OBAMA ADMINISTRATION (2008-2015) 67
   TRUMP ADMINISTRATION (2017-2020) 68
   BIDEN ADMINISTRATION (2021-2024) 71
   TRUMP ADMINISTRATION (2025) 73
   THE STEADY DECAY 74
   ANCIENT EXAMPLES OF INTERNAL DECAY 80

    Modern Examples of Internal Decay 81
    Harnessing Decay 87
    Exploiting a Crisis 89
    An Attempt to Reverse 91

7 SOCIETY ENGINEERED 92

    Characterising the American People 93
    Rights and Freedoms 96
    Every Man for Himself 97
    Normalization of Abuse 99
    Life Expectancy 102
    The Continual Crisis 105
    The American Laboratory 108
    Maslow's Hierarchy of Needs... 110

8 DOOMED NATIONS 117

    The European Downfall is Nigh 118
    The attack 140

9 BREAKING OLD BONDS 146

    Russia's relationships are "complicated" 147
    The global sands are shifting 149
    The World Aligns with Russia and China?.....................154
    The Downstairs Neighbour..158

10 THE FINAL SHIFT 163

    The Fall of the Final Empire 163
    Book of Revelation Prophecy 166
    Who or what is the Antichrist? 170
    The Rise of the Beast 183
    Interwoven Forces deciding our Fate? 187
    The Old gives way to the New... 190

11 REVELATION 192

    Kamala Harris and the Scarf...193
    Just a case of End Times Fascism?.....................................198
    The link between duality and prophecy 212
    The way forward 234

ACKNOWLEDGEMENTS 269

SOURCES AND FURTHER READING 271

Prologue

The sky, neither day nor night, breathes in shifting hues. Violet, amber, and a quiet shade of blue that trembles on the edge of darkness. In this in-between, time falters, bending in silent waves, neither past nor future, neither certain nor unknown. It is twilight.

For those who watch closely, twilight is more than a fleeting moment. It is a threshold, a delicate suspension between forces, a balance held in fragile equilibrium. The ancients saw it in omens scratched into stone. The mystics whispered its name in their prayers. Physicists now trace its echoes in quantum interference, where time itself refracts like light, touching past and future in layered waves. Twilight does not simply mark transition. It is the language of prophecy, whispered from the depths of the unseen, woven through history, myth, and memory.

Truth and lies press close within the half-light, cloaked together in the interplay of dusk and dawn. They exist inseparably, whispering in tandem.

They move like a shadow, elusive yet omnipresent, shifting between revelation and deception. Prophecy emerges in this space. It is born from the interference of moments, from whispers carried across time's undulating fabric. It is in twilight where the warnings appear, the anomalies surface, and history bends toward its foretold fate.

And yet, those who understand twilight know it is both a beginning and an end. It is cyclical yet unbroken, persistent yet imperceptible - a force beyond singularity. It holds the echoes of forgotten gods who ruled in the shifting light, the murmurs of celestial bodies locked in gravitational dance, the silent rhythms of shadowy creatures navigating between existence and obscurity. Time itself breathes within twilight, stretching, folding, unravelling.

Artists paint it in golden hues; poets write its song in verses of longing and revelation. Philosophers wrestle with its paradoxical reality: contradiction does not diminish truth; it defines its very foundation.

Twilight is the bridge between waking thought and subconscious revelation, between logic and instinct, between science and spirit. Its influence creeps into myth, into biology, into dreams. Into language itself and all that exists, twilight speaks in the quiet voice of transition.

Because in the half-light, one finds the space where truth and lies converge, where meaning flickers between certainty and illusion, indistinguishable yet infinite.

And from that convergence, the prophecy emerges.

Introduction

For as long as humanity has existed, we have sought meaning in the unknown. Some turn to science, others to religion, and many to prophecy - the quiet whispers of a world operating beyond our immediate perception.

Prophecy is often dismissed as superstition, reduced to vague predictions or cryptic warnings. But what if prophecy is not merely a forecast of the future? What if it is a message, a thread woven through reality. Could it be that prophecy is inviting us to see, to pay attention, and to understand?

I am not a psychic. I am not a prophet. I am simply someone who began experiencing dreams that held no relevance to my daily life yet somehow aligned with unfolding global events. At first, I dismissed them as strange coincidences. Over time, the patterns became undeniable. Long before the first of these dreams I had spent decades chasing a prophecy that captivated my thoughts. I began to wonder. *What if we have misinterpreted the true purpose of prophecy all along?*

Prophecy may not exist simply to predict events; it may exist to illuminate our ability to shape them. We are often too distracted, too occupied with the mechanics of daily life, to recognize the signals appearing all around us. A fleeting dream. A persistent thought. A moment of déjà vu. Unexplainable emotions. We brush them aside, convinced they are meaningless fragments of experience. But what if they are glimpses into a deeper reality? What if they are invitations to see the world differently - to step beyond the rigid frameworks of science, religion, and psychology and embrace a broader understanding of existence?

The world around us is changing. Political landscapes, societal structures, and even the fabric of human consciousness are shifting. In places like the United States, growing cynicism and a survivalist mindset reinforce a dangerous cycle of domination and exclusion, where fear is weaponized, and collective unity is strategically dismantled. Meanwhile, an elite class works to privatize essential services, deepening the divide between those who control the future and those merely subjected to it. But what if this is part of the illusion? What if the apocalyptic narrative they present is carefully manufactured to ensure compliance? Could the intention be to keep us trapped in a reactive existence rather than an empowered one? Furthermore, does prophecy provide the windows of opportunity through which to escape our entrapment?

Throughout history, humanity has been trained to accept external forces as the architects of our fate. The concept of "chosen ones" has reinforced the idea that only few hold the keys to transformation, while the rest of us wait, hoping for intervention. But this perspective is flawed. We are all chosen. Each of us carries a quantum spark, an inner divinity capable of influencing our shared reality. Whether we acknowledge it or not, we are constantly shaping the future through our thoughts, actions, and intentions. The question is no longer whether we have the power to alter our path - it is whether we will choose to wield that power.

Prophecy is an invitation. It does not dictate a fixed destiny. It outlines possibilities, leaving the final choice to us. If we view prophecy as more than an uncontrollable force, if we recognize it as a series of stepping stones meant for us to decode, then perhaps we hold more power than we have been led to believe. Perhaps our reality is ours to design.

This book is not just an exploration of prophecy; it is a call to action. It invites every reader, regardless of background, belief, or scepticism, to consider a radical idea: that the smallest changes, the tiniest shifts in perception, can ignite a transformation of monumental proportions. A quantum leap beginning at the individual level, can ripple outward. Each ripple serves to alter the trajectory of human evolution itself.

We don't inherit the world, we build it. We don't merely witness prophecy, we shape it. It is time to rewrite the narrative, to reclaim our role in designing the reality that lies ahead.

Chapter One
Genesis

In 2016 I began experiencing a remarkable series of dreams. The dreams prompted me to search for answers. Nine years later and I publicly share my dreams and other findings with thousands of people around the world through my platform, Ellie Dreams Down Under. What began as an exploration of peculiar visions soon converged with a strange prophecy that I encountered in my youth, propelling me into a public-facing role that I never could have anticipated. Through years of research, reflection, and the interwoven threads of esoteric, spiritual, and religious studies, a central theme has emerged - one that challenges the very nature of prophecy itself.

Some of the memories of the prophecy are hazy, others are as clear as though I had read the prophecy a moment ago. Overall, my memories fall into three different categories. There are fragments that I am 100% certain formed part of the prophecy, and these I speak about with confidence as having been foretold, exactly as I describe in this book.

Some fragments are vaguely recalled, but my recollections are not precise, and I am less confident about those memories. I keep these aspects of the prophecy as I remember in my mind and wait to see if they unfold as I believe was foretold.

There are other fragments of the prophecy that I know are in my memory somewhere, but I have trouble reaching them to recall them accurately enough to describe them with a reasonable degree of confidence. These aspects of my recollection of the prophecy may be flawed, and when I refer to these events, places, or entities, I include a caveat to ensure that you, the reader, can be aware that I am not certain if I am remembering phrase or inference correctly.

It is also reasonable to confess to the fact that there were likely to be aspects of the prophecy that I did not sufficiently digest enough to ever remember at all. This is possibly the most infuriating thing for me wrestle with. Did I remember the right parts of the prophecy? Did I simply take in what my brain wanted to acknowledge, and ignore anything worrying for me at the time?

It is important to consider the fact that I was 20 years old with no interest in, or knowledge of, geo-politics when I encountered this prophecy. I doubt that I knew or cared who the Prime Minister of my own country was in that moment, let alone a future President of a faraway country I had never visited. The fact that I even remember that I ever saw a specific prophecy in that moment, regardless of what the prophecy said, is extraordinary. I do remember, and that is perhaps the ironic reason why I can't forget what I saw.

With everything now explained, the prophecy unfolds as I recall it. First, it appears in its entirety, followed by a detailed exploration of each section, allowing its deeper meaning to emerge. Every word is chosen with care to remain as close to my original recollection as possible. To the best of my knowledge its message remains unchanged. untouched by embellishment or reinterpretation.

The Prophecy

The following is a verbatim recollection of the entire prophecy.

> *Shortly following the start of the next millennium, a new American President will be chosen for office. He shall have 5 letters in his last name, and he shall forge an unholy alliance with another world leader who also has 5 letters in his last name.*
>
> *Together, these 2 world leaders will place in motion the deliberate events to destroy the existing world as it is known and replace it with a new world order.*
>
> *The method to achieve this will be twofold. Firstly, to destroy the foundation that gives strength and stability to the West. Secondly, to ignite a conflict, originating in the East in proximity to the Mediterranean Sea, that will spread across the world.*
>
> *Amid steady decay of the United States, many will arrive with the idea of supporting themselves, but one man will reverse his retirement and arrive to support others. He will attempt to reverse the outcome of events.*
>
> *The people will be trained to become like rats.*
>
> *On the day after Europe's downfall, the United States, at its time of greatest weakness, will be attacked on its own soil by Russia and China [and another] for what will be the first time, but not the last.*

The West will align to Russia, the East and Oceania to China. The United States will be alone.

Until the world, as it is known, will be replaced with the New World. And the New World will last beyond the next millennium.

At the time that I read the prophecy so many years ago, I recall that the messages were broken down into sections, which appeared alongside representative images.

In the first section, depicting two world leaders, the imagery included an American flag and a handshake between two white, male hands. One of the hands bore a signet-style ring with a military aesthetic.

Military rings often symbolize pride, honour, and camaraderie, commemorating a soldier's service, achievements, or affiliation with a specific branch, unit, or mission. They also serve as keepsakes, preserving the memory of military service and the deep bonds formed among service members. Some are awarded as tokens of recognition for dedication and accomplishments, carrying personal and historical significance.

In this particular imagery, I acknowledge the inclusion of the military-style ring as a possible visual representation of alliance. The ring appeared to be engraved or embossed like a traditional signet ring. The design may have signified the identity of the other world leader, perhaps incorporating symbols of their nation's flag or other markers of national pride. However, I do not recall the exact design and cannot be certain of its specific meaning.

Similarly, I cannot say with certainty whether this artistic detail was directly relevant to the prophecy, but I suspect it carried significance. It may have been a representation of the leader's nation or the leader himself.

Another section of the prophecy included an image of a mushroom cloud, as would depict a nuclear explosion, or other type of massive bomb event, such as would appear during a military conflict. I do not recall which part of the prophecy this image sat alongside.

These are the only 2 images that I recall from the prophecy. However, there were others, which were positioned alongside relevant sections to help visually demonstrate and emphasize the section's messaging.

The prophecy was printed in colour onto a pamphlet approximately 5 x 4 inches in diameter. The outer pages were of slightly heavier stock than the inner pages, but the paper overall was likely to be a premium grade with satin or gloss finish. The pamphlet had been bound into a thin booklet with staples.

The pamphlet had been professionally printed, by an entity acknowledged on the outer back cover of the booklet. I don't recall the name of the printer.

The only contents of the booklet was the prophecy.

The Life Context

I married young, just nineteen years old. My husband and I had been together since I was sixteen, and we became engaged shortly after my eighteenth birthday. Though our marriage didn't last, he was with me, whether as my fiancé or husband, when I first encountered the prophecy. In fact, we looked at it together and spoke about it briefly, which might explain why its message has stayed with me so vividly and for so long.

The setting was the home of friends. The man was my husband's distant relative, possibly a second or third cousin, living with his long-time girlfriend, who had recently become his fiancée. We sat on their sofa, waiting for them to finish getting ready so the four of us could go out for dinner.

It's odd to think about what I remember and what I don't. Their names have slipped from my mind, perhaps because they were more my husband's friends than mine, and when our marriage ended, they naturally realigned with him. I don't recall where we went that night, what we ate or drank, or whether their relationship endured.

What I do remember, however, is the house. I can still picture it in precise detail. I recall the living room's relationship to the front door, the general colour scheme, the room proportions compared to my own home. The coffee table had a glass top, the sofa was a classic corduroy two-seater, and the house itself was a compact, single-story mid-terrace, wedged into a sharp curve on a busy road. There was no parking out front, but residents could enter through an alleyway in the back.

I recall little about the man beyond his Italian heritage, which he shared with my husband. His fiancée was petite, Australian, with a wild mass of curly chestnut hair. She was a vegetarian, and I had been to the house before, once for a pasta meal that was severely undercooked. We all assured her it was delicious. She was kind and delighted to be hosting one of her first dinner parties, which of course deserved encouragement. Besides, I expect that each of our cooking skills were equally unrefined.

On the evening that I saw the prophecy it was simply sitting there on the coffee table, mixed in with other mail and store catalogues that had likely been pushed through the slot of the front door. Absentmindedly, I picked it up and flicked through its pages, remarking to my husband how melodramatic it was - its vivid imagery, its emotive language. At the time, we laughed about how gullible religious people must be to fall for such doom-laden predictions of the future.

And yet, something held my attention. I read the prophecy cover to cover, studied its imagery, occasionally flipping back to earlier pages to reread what had been written. For a while, I was engrossed. And then, just as suddenly, I lost interest. I tossed it back onto the coffee table and picked up a store catalogue.

Chapter Two
Stagecraft

In the following chapters, I will outline the process by which I have examined the prophecy in depth. First, I explore how its statements are phrased, dissect their definitions and interpretations, and provide examples and sources that have led me to the conclusions presented in this book. The final section offers a summary of my thoughts and ideas on how to move forward.

I am not a historian, theologian, or an expert in prophecy, economics, military strategy, politics, international relations, or any of the diverse fields touched upon by the prophecy. Rather, I am an observer - one who has been studying and contemplating its meanings for approximately 40 years. Throughout this time, I have followed wherever the prophecy seemed to lead, allowing myself to explore every domain it touched.

At times, its connections to domestic and international political events were striking, perhaps even responsible for the unexplained dreams I experienced in my early years of study. Now that I am publicly engaged and in conversation with an audience who frequently share their own experiences, I have come to realize that many others have had peculiar dreams tied to themes like my own. As we collectively witness a far-reaching crisis unfold - both in the United States and beyond - it is possible that the weight of stress and anxiety, particularly for those who feel an impending sense of dread, has contributed to the emergence of this collective dream phenomenon in recent years.

Over time, the boundaries between politics, history, and esotericism have begun to blur. There have been countless days when I have wondered how I could be the only person recognizing the intricate links between seemingly disparate concepts - crisis-driven news cycles, culture wars, religion and faith, unexplained phenomena, ancient teachings, indigenous folklore, geopolitics, psychology, and science. The connections between them may not be as arbitrary as they first appear.

This book is my attempt to follow the breadcrumbs scattered across these disciplines and demonstrate that they may not be as disconnected as we are led to believe. In fact, they could be converging toward a singular reality - one that is waiting to reveal itself in due time. Whether that revelation unfolds depends on our willingness to recognize and follow the clues laid before us.

Over time, I have come to believe that these clues are not merely coincidences but offerings - guiding markers that invite us to acknowledge and engage with them. In doing so, we unlock one of the most powerful tools at our disposal: the ability to anticipate and recalibrate our future with greater awareness and intention.

I am fully aware that I may have made mistakes along the way. Some interpretations may be flawed, and some observations incomplete. I am not an insider, nor do I claim expertise in the subjects I discuss.

This book does not seek to provide a definitive, authoritative, or perfectly precise account of historical figures, personalities, relationships, or motivations. Rather, it is a collection of my reflections and an exploration of how these observations have come to shape my understanding.

Ultimately, I invite you, the reader, to embark on this journey with me, to examine my observations, and to reach your own independent conclusions.

Chapter Three
The Millennium Pact

> *Shortly following the start of the next millennium, a new American President will be chosen for office. He shall have 5 letters in his last name, and he shall forge an unholy alliance with another world leader who also has 5 letters in his last name.*

What makes this prophecy truly remarkable is how it unfolded. The precise timing of the new president's arrival, the exact number of letters in his name, and the powerful alliance he would forge with another world leader - these intricately woven details seized my attention immediately. Unlike any prophecy I had encountered before, this one distinguished itself through a compelling "hook" that not only captivated me but also etched itself permanently into my memory.

The new American President

The term "American President" is generally understood to refer specifically to the President of the United States of America, and the title "President" denotes the head of state and government of that country.

However, if we consider the broader context, the term "American" could theoretically refer to individuals from the continents of North and South America. In this very broad sense, the term "American President" could apply to the president of any country such as Brazil, Argentina or Canada. But is it reasonable to assume that this was the case for this prophecy? No, it isn't.

Many across the American continent feel frustrated when "American" is used solely for US citizens, despite rarely claiming the term themselves, instead embracing national identities like Argentinian, Brazilian, or Colombian. Thus, the prophecy evidently referred to the President of the United States.

The prophecy was also clearly identifying the President to be male, and that his alliance would be established with another male world leader.

The term "new American President" indicates that the individual would not be an incumbent president seeking re-election as at the start of the "next millennium". Their entrance into office would represent a "new" presidency. Each millennium begins on the 1st day of the 1st month, immediately following the end of the thousandth calendar year. Hence, the prophecy was referring to the millennium which began on January 1st, 2001.

The Man with 5 Letters in his Name

To qualify for the prophecy, the US President must have "5 letters in his last name". He must "be chosen for office" which is a term that implies entrance via the presidential election process, but alternatively by some other type of transfer of power. The "choice" to transfer the power of the presidency to this individual may belong to US voters. Alternatively, and rather curiously, the prophecy's phrasing of this section implies that a choice may be made by someone or something other than US voters. It seems an innocent choice of words when relevant to events such as the transfer of power to President Johnson following President Kennedy's assassination, or to President Ford following President Nixon's resignation. However, the choice of words is peculiar once the prophesied millennium begins, considering the individuals who were ultimately "chosen" to be US President.

To illustrate the unique US presidential qualities set forth by the prophecy, it is helpful to go further back in time than simply the turn of the millennium. And so, I did exactly that, searching as far back as 1950. Using the two-party political system adopted by the United States since the 1800s, I compared the criteria set by the prophecy against every President, Vice President and opposing party candidate, in every instance in which a "new" president was "chosen for office". I included every transfer of power, whether due to election result, resignation or assassination. The results were remarkable. To illustrate, the names of the individuals who meet the criteria of the prophecy are highlighted with **bold** lettering.

Candidates relevant to the prior millennium

In 1953, Dwight Eisenhower became the new US President. His Vice President was **Richard Nixon**. The opposing candidate was Adlai Stevenson.

In 1961, John F. Kennedy commenced presidential office. Kennedy's Vice President was Lyndon Johnson, and his opponent was **Richard Nixon**. In 1963, following Kennedy's assassination, Lyndon Johnson became the new US President, with Hubert Humphrey assuming the role of Vice President. Johnson was elected to a full term thereafter. His opponent was Barry Goldwater.

Richard Nixon became the new US President in 1969. His Vice President was **Spiro Agnew**, who was replaced in 1973 by Gerald Ford. Nixon had 2 opposing candidates, Hubert Humphrey in the first cycle, and George McGovern in this second. After Nixon resigned from office in 1974, Gerald Ford became the new US President. His Vice President was Nelson Rockefeller.

In 1977 Jimmy Carter became the new US President, with Walter Mondale serving as Vice President, and Gerald Ford as opposing candidate.

In 1981, Ronald Reagan became the new US President. His Vice President was George H.W. Bush, and the opposing candidates were Jimmy Carter in the first cycle, followed by Walter Mondale in the second.

George H.W. Bush became the new US President in 1989, with J. Danford Quayle serving as Vice President. Michael Dukakis was the opposing candidate.

In 1994, Bill Clinton became the new US President. His Vice President was Al Gore, and the opposing candidates were George H.W. Bush in the first cycle, and Bob Dole in the second.

Observably, the only candidate who met the criteria of having 5 letters in his last name over the period of 50 years prior to the commencement of the present millennium, was **Richard Nixon**. It is also notable that Nixon's Vice President, **Spiro Agnew**, also had 5 letters in his name. The Vice President is "chosen" to serve as back-up President in the event the incumbent President is unable to serve for any reason. This places Agnew in a position of prophetic credibility, like Nixon.

Whilst a few lesser-known candidates ran for office during this 50-year period, the likelihood of their election to office was slim. The US election process is dominated by the 2-party system, which significantly diminishes the chance for any 3rd party candidate to realistically enter office. Of the credible contenders, no other individuals met the criteria of the prophecy.

Candidates relevant to the prophesied millennium

George W. Bush entered Presidential Office in 2001. His Vice President was Dick Cheney. The opposing candidates were Al Gore in the first cycle, and **John Kerry** in the second.

In 2009, **Barack Obama** became US President. His Vice President was **Joe Biden** during both terms in office. The opposing candidates were John McCain in the first cycle, and Mitt Romney in the second.

Donald Trump entered Presidential Office in 2017, with **Mike Pence** acting as Vice President. The opposing candidate was Hillary Clinton.

In 2021, **Joe Biden** commenced in office. Kamala Harris was the US Vice President. The opposing candidate was **Donald Trump**.

In 2025, **Donald Trump** returned to Presidential Office, with Vice President **J.D. Vance**. The opposing candidate was initially **Joe Biden**, but 15 weeks prior to the election, Biden stepped down from his campaign and nominated Kamala Harris as his replacement.

The most notable shift in elections following the commencement of the new millennium, is frequency with which credible candidates for the US Presidency have 5 letters in their last names. The first cycle, involving Bush and Kerry marks the beginning of this phenomena, which then continues uninterrupted to the current day.

Although George W. Bush officially took office after the turn of the millennium, his selection occurred prior to the shift, technically placing his first presidency within the previous millennial framework. His second term, however, does not meet the same criteria, regardless of his name, By the time he sought re-election, he was no longer a "new" president.

The first election cycle in which a truly new president could have emerged featured **John Kerry** as the notable candidate. Kerry, whose last name consists of five letters, would have qualified had he been chosen for the presidency. Kerry was not ultimately chosen for the Presidency.

It is also worth noting that the Bush vs. Kerry election had the second-tightest Electoral College margin in recent history (286–251), surpassed only by the previous election cycle between Bush and Gore, which was ultimately decided by the Supreme Court ruling in *Bush v. Gore* (271–266). In fact, both election wins by George W. Bush were strongly disputed. The first cycle resulted in a recounting of the Florida votes, and a subsequent legal battle that resulted in the Supreme Court of the United States deciding the outcome of the election. The events made the 2000 election cycle and the victory of President Bush one of the most disputed elections in modern history.

The following cycle was marked by several controversies, particularly regarding the voting process. Key issues included widespread complains about voting difficulties and long voter lines and wait times, voter suppression complaints, voter registration issues, and electronic voting concerns. In Ohio, there were also allegations of election fraud, where exit polls initially suggested a win by Kerry. This led to other allegations of voting irregularities and fraud in several states.

In the context of the prophecy, had John Kerry won Ohio and its 20 electoral votes he would have secured the 271 needed to claim the US presidency. This pivotal scenario is one that my research has identified as a potential "clue."

Upon closer examination, the prophecy appears to be intricately tied to events within its foretold timeframe, particularly those that are unusual, controversial, or highly contested. The Kerry defeat in 2004 marks the first in a sequence of phenomena that I have pinpointed as possible prophetic indicators.

When all post-millennial presidential cycles are considered, a compelling question arises: Was the Bush v. Kerry election in 2004 a symbolic clue regarding the prophecy's deeper purpose? This is a question I examine in more detail later in this book.

Once the new millennium began, the first individual to enter office as a new president was **Barack Obama** who was elected in 2008. After Obama, the next new president was **Donald Trump** in 2016. After Trump, **Joe Biden** was elected as a new president in 2020. After Biden, **Donald Trump** was elected for the second time. Interestingly, he was elected again, as a "new" president. Trump is currently the President of the United States. If he were to depart the presidency before the end of his current term, **J D Vance** would enter as a new president. Just like in his earlier term, when **Mike Pence** was Vice President, President Trump's Vice President, acting as back-up to the President, has 5 letters in his last name.

Furthermore, during Donald Trump's first term as President, several attempts were made to remove him from office before the end of his term. In 2019, the US House of Representatives initiated an impeachment attempt over allegations that Trump had abused his power by pressuring the President of Ukraine, Volodymyr Zelensky, to investigate his political opponent Joe Biden, along with Mr Biden's son. The impeachment and conviction processes comprise 2 parts. The impeachment, a process undertaken by the House, acts as a mark against the individual who has been impeached. A conviction is voted on separately in the US Senate and can prevent the individual from serving in public office entirely. The House voted to impeach Trump, but the Senate acquitted him in early 2020.

In 2021, following the January 6 Capitol attack, the House impeached Trump for a second time. Whilst Trump was no longer President at the time of the impeachment, an impeachment conviction could have prevented him from entering public office later. Once again, the Senate voted not to convict.

Throughout Trump's first term as President, US lawmakers and public officials regularly suggested invoking the 25th Amendment of the United State Constitution, which allows for the removal of a president deemed unable to perform their duties. However, this was never formally pursued.

If any of these attempts to remove Trump from office had succeeded, his Vice President, Mike Pence, would have taken his place. Pence, whose last name also has 5 letters, would enter office as a new president, and thus would immediately meet the criteria of the prophecy.

The nature that every US President who entered office as a new president following the start of the millennium, has had 5 letters in his last name and thus met each of the criteria of the prophecy, is exceptional. Equally exceptional is the frequency with which the Vice Presidents and campaign opponents have also had 5 letters in their last name.

A Remarkable Presidential Election cycle

A notable exception is Kamala Harris who was Joe Biden's Vice President, and a last-minute Presidential opponent to Donald Trump during the 2024 presidential election. Harris experienced a meteoric rise in popularity during the 107 days of her campaign, capturing significant attention as the first Black and South Asian woman to lead a major party ticket. Her campaign's dynamic momentum, however, was short-lived and Donald Trump ultimately secured victory.

Whilst there is no factual basis from which to draw, I have often wondered whether Harris failed to win the election, simply because she did not meet the criteria set by the prophecy. This might seem like an oversimplified notion at this point of the book, but as events unfold it proves itself to be a more and more curious circumstance. The conditions that initiated her campaign were sufficiently outside of the norm to raise questions pertaining to her place in the prophecy. Was she an unforeseen risk to a series of events destined to take place?

To illustrate my point, consider that Kamala Harris became the Democratic presidential candidate in 2024 under unusual circumstances. On July 21, 2024, President Joe Biden unexpectedly withdrew his bid for re-election and endorsed Harris on the same day. This abrupt shift left Harris with a condensed timeline to prepare her campaign. Harris's nomination process was highly unusual compared to the norm. Typically, presidential candidates secure their party's nomination through a lengthy primary process involving debates, state-by-state voting, and delegate accumulation. In Harris's case, she appeared in a manner that was a surprise to her own party. This rapid and unconventional set of circumstances sets Harris's nomination apart from the traditional process.

Kamala Harris became Mr Trump's unexpected presidential opponent amid concerns about Joe Biden's age and perceived mental acuity. Biden's performance in a debate with Trump raised doubts about his ability to effectively campaign and govern, leading to increased pressure from within his party to step aside. Additionally, economic challenges, including inflation and public dissatisfaction with his handling of the economy, further weakened his position as a candidate. These factors collectively contributed to his decision to withdraw from the race and endorse Kamala Harris as the Democratic nominee. However, days prior to his endorsement of Harris, President Biden was fervently proclaiming his intention to run for a second term. This raises another question: Despite the concerns circulating at the time, is it possible that Joe Biden was the prophecy's intended winner of the 2024 presidential election? Mr Biden also meets the criteria of another aspect of the prophecy, to be discussed later in this book.

The Kamala Harris factor is a unique one that, for various reasons, might provide an important clue about the prophecy that warrants closer examination.

An Unholy Alliance

The term "unholy alliance" is an idiomatic expression used to describe a partnership or coalition that appears highly unusual, counter-intuitive, or even morally repugnant. It brings together parties that, by their very nature, would be expected to oppose one another.

There are a variety of ways in which the term "unholy alliance" may be used. In the general context, it relates to an unexpected partnership between typically opposing groups, which is marked by moral or ethical disapproval. The alliance may be seen as suspicious or dangerous because the joining forces traditionally compete or undercut one another. Their alliance compromises each party's principles or integrity. An example in the general context may include rival companies that suddenly join forces. Whereas they were previously known for engaging in cutthroat competitor tactics, they suddenly rally together to dominate the market.

The political or societal context may give rise to an unholy alliance. In this example, a strategic partnership or coalition of groups with divergent ideologies may form, which triggers suggestions of opportunism. Opposing social action groups may set aside their ideological differences to jointly oppose a political opponent or government policy. Suspicions may arise because the partnership potentially undermines democratic values or public trust.

In the context of religion and morality, a union viewed as sacrilegious may occur. In this example, religious leaders may exchange favours and influence with immoral or unethical business or political leaders. The alliance is marked as fundamentally antithetical to accepted moral or religious doctrines, and defiant of divine or sacred precepts.

There is also a type of unholy alliance pertaining to the literary or artistic context. It involves a dramatic description of menacing alliance formed by unlikely partners or a bizarre set of conflicting character traits. It may involve a story in which the plot centres around evil creatures who conspire against a heroic figure. Alternatively, it may point to a morally ambiguous character who evokes a sense of loathing whilst somehow also being strangely magnetic or intriguing.

A well-known fictional character who meets this last set of criteria is Hannibal Lecter from the film, *The Silence of the Lambs*. Lecter is undeniably brilliant, cultured and charismatic, qualities that make him strangely compelling. Yet, his cold-blooded nature and cannibalistic tendencies make him deeply unsettling and repulsive.

One historical example of an unholy alliance is the Molotov-Ribbentrop Pact of 1939. This was a non-aggression treaty between Nazi Germany and the Soviet Union, two ideologically opposed regimes. The pact shocked the world because it brought together Adolf Hitler's fascist Germany and Joseph Stalin's communist Union of Soviet Socialist Republics (USSR). The two powers that had previously been bitter enemies.

The agreement included secret protocols dividing Eastern Europe into spheres of influence, leading to the invasion and partition of Poland. The alliance was seen as "unholy" because it was a pragmatic, opportunistic move that disregarded the profound ideological differences between the two regimes. It ultimately facilitated the outbreak of World War II and had devastating consequences for the countries involved. The Pact of 1939 is particularly interesting because it aligns to another aspect of the prophecy which will be discussed later in this book.

There is a prophesied entity who is widely considered to possess the traits that render him unholy in the contexts of literature and art, religion and morality, plus society and politics. This entity is the Antichrist of biblical acclaim, who includes the unique quality of having an "unholy" characteristic of simultaneous repulsion and fascination. The Antichrist is also examined in closer detail later in this book.

The Second Thread

One of the most striking aspects of the prophecy is its specificity when it comes to the 2 allied world leaders. As was shown earlier in this chapter, the introduction of US Presidents with 5 letters in their last names, suddenly became a constant, immediately upon the first election for a new president after the shift in millennium.

Equally striking is the specificity of referencing "another world leader" to which the US President will enjoy an unholy alliance. The other world leader must also be a male with 5 letters in his last name to meet the criteria of the prophecy.

It is difficult to know whether any former US Presidents fashioned a notable alliance with another world leader over the course of his presidency that would meet the criteria of "unholy" as contextualized in this book. Commonly known alliances, along with some of the lesser-known examples are examinable.

Barack Obama (2009-2017)

To my knowledge, as an interested observer who does not have affiliation or direct/indirection connection to US politics, I have been able to identify what I believe are the most notable "alliances" that were made between President Obama and other world leaders.

The German Chancellor, Angela Merkel, was one of Obama's closest allies, particularly on issues like climate change and global security.

The Japanese Prime Minister, Shinzo Abe, worked closely with the US President on strengthening the US-Japan alliance and addressing challenges in the Asia-Pacific region.

The British Prime Minister, David Cameron, shared a strong partnership with Obama, especially on counterterrorism and economic matters.

The Canadian Prime Minister, Justin Trudeau, shared the President's values on matters of climate action and progressive policies.

President Obama collaborated with the French President, Francois Hollande, on matters of counterterrorism and the Paris Climate Agreement.

The Israeli Prime Minister, Benjamin Netanyahu, had a complex relationship with President Obama, but they worked closely on Middle Eastern policy and shared security concerns.

None of these world leaders have 5 letters in their last name. Arguably the US President's closest foreign ally at the time, Angela Merkel, is also female and therefore immediately disqualified. So, without another individual appearing to fit the criteria of notably allied to Barack Obama, the path of enquiry appears to stop here.

Donald Trump (2017-2020)

The entire world witnessed a different style of leadership when Donald Trump first took office in January 2017. It was often difficult to ascertain where his alliances lay with most of the following examples. Nonetheless, several leaders stood out as having significant rapport with Trump in his first term.

The Israeli Prime Minister, Benjamin Netanyahu shared a strong alignment with President Trump, particularly on matters relating to the Abraham Accord, and moving the US embassy to Jerusalem.

The Russian President, Vladimir Putin had a notably unusual relationship with the US President. It was characterized by a mix of public admiration from Donald Trump towards President Putin. This was mixed with attempts to improve US-Russia relations despite longstanding geopolitical tension and ongoing controversies surrounding the topic of election interference. Donald Trump's decision to publicly side with Vladimir Putin over US intelligence agencies during their 2018 Helsinki summit was an extraordinary departure from traditional American foreign policy, sparking widespread criticism and raising questions about his approach to adversarial relations, The relationship dynamic between Trump and Putin often blurred the lines between adversarial and cooperative, making it a relationship that defied traditional diplomatic norms.

The British Prime Minister, Theresa May, had a working relationship with President Trump that emphasized the "special relationship" between the US and UK. May was the first foreign leader to visit Trump after his inauguration, where she secured his commitment to NATO. They also collaborated on defence and security, such as the joint bombing campaign in Syria following chemical attacks. However, their alliance faced challenges, including disagreements over tariffs and Trump's controversial actions, which sometimes strained their rapport.

The Indian Prime Minister, Narendra Modi, fostered a positive relationship with President Trump, focusing on trade and defence cooperation. There were also other leaders, who had notable interactions with Trump that could fall under the banner of an "alliance".

The North Korean leader, Kim Jong Un had unprecedented meetings with President Trump, including one in which Trump crossed the border into North Korea to meet Kim Jong Un in his own country. This act by President Trump marked the first time a sitting US president set foot in the country, symbolizing an unprecedented moment in diplomatic history and a bold attempt to ease decades of hostility.

The Saudi Crown Prince, Mohammed bin Salman, also shared an unusual and close relationship with President Trump, particularly on arms deals and Middle East policies. Trump broke tradition once again in his relationship with the Crown Prince, by being the first US president to choose Saudi Arabia for his inaugural foreign trip, emphasizing a strategic focus on Gulf partnerships and Middle Eastern diplomacy.

The Brazilian President, Jair Bolsonaro, aligned with President Trump on conservative values and trade discussions. The two men appeared to share a unique bond, resulting in them often being referred to as "ideological twins", united by their nationalist agendas, anti-establishment rhetoric and mutual admiration for each other's leadership styles.

The relationships between President Trump and foreign "allies", while significant, often differed in tone and substance to allied relationships fostered by other US Presidents. Traditionally, alliances were rooted in multilateral cooperation and shared democratic values. Trump's alliances appeared on the face to be transactional and centred on specific interests.

The notable relationship with the US President during this time was that with Russia's President, Vladimir Putin, who has 5 letters in his last name.

Joe Biden (2021-2025)

During Joe Biden's presidency, his foreign alliances have been marked by a focus on rebuilding trust and multilateral cooperation. Most of the following examples represented Biden's concerted effort to restore foreign relationships that had been achieved between former President Barack Obama, during which Mr Biden had served as Vice President and was no doubt already a key part of those established relationships, some of which had deteriorated or faded during the Trump presidency.

The Ukrainian President, Volodymyr Zelensky, has been a key ally, with President Biden providing significant military and financial support during an ongoing conflict between Ukraine and Russia.

The French President, Emmanuel Macron shared a strong partnership with President Biden, particularly on matters of climate change and the US commitment to NATO.

The German Chancellor, Olaf Scholz, worked closely with President Biden to maintain European security (and the public sense of US-led solidarity), and energy policies.

The Indian Prime Minister, Narendra Modi was a vital partner with Biden in strengthening the "Quad" alliance. The Quad, officially known as the Quadrilateral Security Dialogue, is a strategic partnership between Australia, India, Japan, and the United States. It focuses on promoting a free, open, and inclusive Indo-Pacific region and addresses key issues like maritime security, climate change, critical technologies, and disaster relief. The Quad is not a military alliance, but rather a platform for multi-national cooperation on matters that provide mutual, wide-ranging support for member nations.

Joe Biden's alliances reflected his emphasis on democratic values and collective action, contrasting with the more transactional approach of Donald Trump's first period in office. In addition to the above, Biden was a consistent partner to the Canadian Prime Minister, Justin Trudeau, Australia's Prime Minister, Anthony Albanese, and the Japanese Prime Minister, Fumio Kishida. Each of these relationships focused on strengthening trade relations, working to combat climate change, and demonstrating shared democratic values.

Whilst President Biden may have communicated or negotiated with other world leaders, of the ones he was observably close to, none are men with 5 letters in their last name.

Donald Trump (2025)

Whilst President Trump's second term in office has been brief at the time of writing, a few notable relationships with foreign leaders appear to stand out as potentially worthy of examination.

During his first presidency, Trump forged alliances with Vladimir Putin, Benjamin Netanyahu, Mohammed bin Salman and Jair Bolsonaro, the leaders of Russia, Israel, Saudi Arabia and Brazil respectively. These relationships were described as they related to President Trump's first term in office and appear to have continued similarly.

In addition to the above, the Hungarian Prime Minister, Viktor Orbán has emerged as a notable ally of Donald Trump, particularly in this second term. Trump has praised Orbán as a "great man" and expressed admiration for his leadership style. Their relationship is marked by shared nationalist values and mutual support, with Orbán reportedly working behind the scenes to bolster Trump's political strategies. This alliance reflects a deep ideological alignment. During Trump's first term, he and Viktor Orbán shared a supportive relationship, marked by mutual admiration for their nationalist policies and conservative values. Orbán publicly endorsed Trump and praised his leadership, while Trump reciprocated by highlighting Orbán's strong stance on issues like migration and sovereignty.

It has, however, become increasingly clear since the end of Donald Trump's first term, that the Orbán alliance is stronger than previously acknowledged.

Timeline of observable bond-making

Donald Trump and Viktor Orbán's alliance became increasingly evident during Trump's first term and solidified further in the years that followed. Due to the ongoing political debate and critiquing of Trump's relationship with the Russian President, other growing alliances took secondary place with news reporters and commentators, however the bond between the 2 men can retrospectively be observed as having occurred with a notable timeline.

Orbán's public endorsement of Trump during the 2016 US presidential campaign appeared to mark the beginning of their alignment. By May 13, 2019, Orbán visited the White House, where Trump praised him as a leader who had "kept [his] country safe". This meeting underscored their shared nationalist and conservative values.

Donald Trump's Republican Party embraced Orbán with increasing pronouncement in subsequent years. In August 2022, Orbán was a featured speaker at the Conservative Political Action Conference (CPAC) in Dallas, Texas, where he was celebrated by American conservatives for his anti-immigration policies and "illiberal democracy" approach. This event highlighted Orbán's growing influence within US conservative circles.

By 2024, Orbán's relationship with Mr Trump deepened further. Reports indicated that Orbán had been actively working behind the scenes to support Trump's re-election campaign. Following Trump's victory in the 2024 election, Orbán publicly announced "big plans" for their collaboration, signalling a defining partnership for Trump's second term.

These developments illustrate how their alliance evolved from mutual admiration to a strategic partnership, with Orbán becoming a symbol of the Republican Party's ideological shift toward embracing leaders with authoritarian tendencies.

Of the 4 presidencies that form the entire group of "new" presidents since the start of the "new millennium" as foretold by the prophecy, only two world leaders appear to fit the prophecy's criteria. Vladimir **Putin** of Russia and Viktor **Orbán** of Hungary are both men with 5 letters in their last name, who forge an alliance with the US President who also has 5 letters his last name. It is reasonable to describe their alliances with the President as fitting the definition of "unholy" as provided earlier in this chapter.

These alliances also represent a previously unthinkable shift for the United States of America, as the international leading national for the promotion of democratic values, towards non-democratic or authoritarian values. This alignment to the prophecy is a prominent feature that for some readers may be perceived as uncanny.

The 1972 Peculiarity

I am aware of an exceptional moment in recent history which took place between the US President and a foreign "allied" leader, and which sits outside the scope of the prophecy. It involved US President Nixon's visit to China in 1972. Nixon was, just as Trump was with North Korea, the first US president to set foot in the People's (Communist) Republic of China.

The Chinese Premier at the time was Zhou Enlai. Nixon's respect for Zhou was evident in his efforts to establish diplomatic relations and his acknowledgment of Zhou's leadership in navigating complex international dynamics. This admiration was part of a broader strategy to reshape US-China relations during the Cold War.

Nixon's approach, like Trump's, was unconventional and marked a significant shift in foreign policy. I find this moment in history to be interesting and potentially relevant to the prophecy for two reasons.

Firstly, as was discussed earlier, Richard Nixon is the only US President to have 5 letters in his last name since 1950, other than every new president to enter office since the commencement of foretold timeline of the prophecy. Whilst the Chinese Premier's family name is Zhou, the Chinese place the family name first when addressing a person's full name. It is therefore correct to address the Premier as "Zhou Enlai", in which his "last name" contains 5 letters.

The visit by President Nixon to China was history making due to its unorthodoxy. Its stark departure from tradition, and the President's public display of admiration for a foreign leader whose values were in direct opposition to that of the United States's position as leading nation on democratic values, could align with the prophecy's articulation of an "unholy alliance". The obvious question in my mind is whether there is a relevance here?

Richard Nixon and the Watergate Scandal gave rise to questions about the strengths and consistencies of US governmental checks and balances. Nixon resigned from the Office of President to avoid criminal indictment on corruption-related charges. He was subsequently afforded a Presidential Pardon by his successor and thereby escaped any process of justice.

Was Nixon a trial run of events foretold to occur in the future? Was the Nixon presidency an opportunity to forestall or prevent the events described in the prophecy entirely? And if so, did the United States fail a test that would have prevented the prophecy altogether? I am not attempting to present this anomaly as evidence of something true. However, I do consider it to be a most peculiar thing, which I cannot ignore. How unlikely is it that the only US President to have 5 letters in his last name during the 50 years prior to the millennium, would also have an alliance qualified to be "unholy" with another world leader with 5 letters in his last name? And yet, it appears to have occurred. Is it another clue?

Chapter Four
Architects of Chaos

> *Together, these 2 world leaders will place in motion the deliberate events to destroy the existing world as it is known and replace it with a new world order.*

This section of the prophecy makes clear that the leadership alliance is formed with a purpose in mind. The purpose is to replace the existing world [order] with an alternative. The purpose is described as "deliberate", meaning that it is intended to result in destruction and replacement of what exists at that time.

Following the end of the Second World War, the world order remained largely unchanged by the time I encountered the prophecy. The fundamental elements of this order - particularly those most relevant to the prophecy - are as follows:

Distribution of Power

This is how power (military, economic, political) is spread among nations. Some periods in history have featured a dominant nation of power. Examples include the Western Roman Empire (1-475 approx.), the British Empire (1588-1947 approx.), and the United States as hegemonic superpower following World War Two

Other periods have been characterised by a multipolar distribution of power. An example of this occurred immediately following the end of the Napoleonic War in 1814. The Concert of Europe was established between the United Kingdom, France, Austria, Prussia, and Russia. Its purpose was to manage the balance of power between nations, and to maintain stability and prevent any single nation from dominating the European continent. This multipolar system for approximately 100 years, until the outbreak of World War One in 1914.

Institutions and Norms

The United Nations, World Bank and International Monetary Fund are all examples of global institutions in which the United States, as hegemonic superpower, led in their creation. Traditions and rules related to international relationships and acceptable treatment of world citizens include diplomatic protocols, human rights, and trade rules. The norms are crucial methods of regulating the way in which nations interact with each other and set standards within which each nation must treat its own citizens, and the citizens of other nations. Not every nation agrees to abide by the norms of the hegemonic superpower, however, the nations that wish to be accepted into global institutions led by such a superpower are generally expected to demonstrate progress towards achieving the standards set by these norms.

The North Atlantic Treaty Organisation (NATO) alliance, and historical conflicts between Ukraine and Russia can be used to better illustrate the concepts of institutions and norms as they relate to world order.

The nation of Ukraine first publicly expressed its interest in becoming a member of NATO in 2002. Before being accepted, Ukraine was expected to demonstrate significant democratic progress by implementing comprehensive reforms in various sectors. This included strengthening the rule of law, ensuring free and fair elections, combating corruption, and enhancing transparency and accountability in governance. Additionally, Ukraine needed to align its military and security sectors with NATO standards, improve human rights protections, and foster a stable and inclusive political environment. These efforts were aimed at ensuring that Ukraine met the democratic and security criteria required for NATO membership.

Russia has also expressed interest in entering NATO. For example, during a January 2001 meeting with then outward-bound President, Bill Clinton, Russian President, Vladimir Putin mentioned the possibility of Russia becoming a member of NATO. Whilst Mr Clinton expressed "no objection" to the idea, the entire US delegation reportedly became very nervous. Russia has subsequently not been accepted into NATO due to historical tensions, conflicting geopolitical interests, security concerns, and significant political differences. NATO states that its primary goal is to ensure collective defence and promote democratic values among its member states. Russia's actions, such as the annexation of Crimea in 2014 and the invasion of Ukraine in 2022, have been viewed as aggressive and destabilizing. This conflicts with

NATO's principles of peace and security and contributes to a complex and often adversarial relationship between NATO and Russia. This makes Russia's potential for NATO membership highly unlikely.

Ideological and Cultural Values

Nations with shared beliefs and ideologies, whether they are liberal democratic in nature, or nationalistic in nature, shape the rules and expectations that govern global conduct. A shift in the values of a dominant nation, can shift the balance of the entire world.

The Protestant Reformation of the 16th century is an example of a shift in cultural and ideological values that caused a domino effect shift in world order. Initiated by Martin Luther's Ninety-Five Theses in 1517, the Reformation challenged the authority and practices of the Roman Catholic Church, leading to the rise of Protestantism. This religious upheaval not only transformed the religious landscape of Europe but also had profound political, social, and economic consequences. It weakened the Catholic Church's dominance, led to the rise of nation-states, and contributed to the development of modern secular governance. The resulting conflicts and realignments significantly altered the balance of power in Europe, paving the way for the emergence of new political entities and a more fragmented, multipolar world order.

Economic Systems and Global Interdependence

The integration of national economies into a global system creates a network of dependencies and incentives that can both stabilize and destabilize international relations.

Trade agreements and global supply chains are examples of global interdependence in which the natural resources of various countries may be used in manufacturing by other countries, which then supply components or finished goods to even more countries. Each participating country is benefiting from the inward-outward shared independence with other participating countries.

Economic systems that help to balance world order may differ across nations. Some examples include the "mixed economy" framework adopted by the United States, Germany and France, which all operate under a cooperative blend of both capitalism and socialism, to balance free markets and government intervention. Also, the "market economy" framework that the United States and Singapore rely upon, is where supply and demand is the determinant of production and prices.

To fully understand the significance of the prophecy, take account of these key components of world order. The "deliberate" events to destroy the "existing world" and replace with a "new world order", is directed towards a deliberate destruction of power distribution, institutions, norms, values, and operating systems.

Chapter Five
The Cradles Ignite

> *The method to achieve this will be twofold. Firstly, to destroy the foundation that gives strength and stability to the West. Secondly, to ignite a conflict, originating in the East in proximity to the Mediterranean Sea, that will spread across the world.*

This section of the prophecy includes 2 parts. The former part refers to a destabilization of "the West", by destroying the "foundation" of its strength. The West is a broad term that is likely to have evolved over time. At the time of writing this book, it generally refers to a group of nations in Western Europe and North America that are characterized by their shared cultural, historical, political and economic traits. This is typically broken down as follows:

Historical and Cultural Roots

The nations that constitute the West have developed from a common heritage which stems from Greco-Roman civilization and Judeo-Christian values. Periods of cultural evolution have helped to define the

West in distinct ways. For example, the Renaissance (1100-1600 approx.) was a revival of classical art, science, and philosophy in Europe that emphasized humanism and critical inquiry. It reshaped Western culture by fostering innovations in art, literature, and science, laying the intellectual and cultural foundations for Western nations.

Another example is the Enlightenment (1650-1800 approx.) which was a transformative intellectual movement that championed reason, science, and individual rights, challenging traditional authorities and inspiring democratic principles, secular governance, and progressive social values that continue to define the West.

Geo-political Identity

The term "the West" is sometimes used to create the perception of a dividing line between the political ideologies, economic models and cultural norms of various countries. The counter term is "the East", which generally encompasses many nations situated in East, South and South-East Asia, plus the Middle East. There are exceptions, the most notable being Israel. Geographically, Israel is in the Middle East and is thus part of the broader "East." However, culturally, politically, and economically, Israel is frequently associated with "the West." In this regard, the commonly shared values and overall outlook on global affairs weighs heavily in determining whether a nation forms part of the West, or the East.

Political and Economic Systems

Countries forming part of "the West" employ or actively strive towards concepts of liberal democracy, the rule of law, and market-based economies. This grouping often includes, but is not limited to, the United States, Canada, the United Kingdom, France, Germany and extends to include Australia and New Zealand.

Many scholars argue that the most "foundational" aspect of "the West" is its commitment to the principles of individual liberty and democratic governance. This core element is rooted in the legacy of ancient Greek philosophy, the rule of law of the Roman tradition, and was later solidified during the Enlightenment through reason, humanism, and scientific inquiry. Confidence in the principles of liberty and democracy has shaped Western political and social institutions. These values underpin free expression, the protection of human rights, and the idea that government accountability is what forms the bedrock of Western identity.

In this context, to "destroy the foundation" of the West means to destroy the mechanisms by which the individual liberties of citizens and democratic protections are maintained. The result, should this occur, would be increased authoritarianism, reduced political freedom, social unrest, economic decline, and potential human rights abuses. The checks and balances that once existed would be lost and replaced with increased corruption and lack of government accountability.

There is substantial evidence that the erosion of individual liberties and democratic protections tends to make a country significantly weaker. Citizen inclusivity is key to a nation's long-term prosperity and stability, whilst marginalisation of broad citizen groups is linked to economic stagnation and social unrest. Studies consistently show that countries with strong democratic frameworks have markedly better outcomes in economic growth, innovation, and political stability compared to authoritarian regimes.

Since the mid-20th century, the United States has generally been considered the leading nation in the West due to its significant influence on global politics, economics and culture. It is reasonable to conclude therefore, that the "foundation" referred to in the prophecy is the democratic, Judeo-Christian foundation of the United States, without which the entire West would suffer instability and democratic decline.

Cracks in the Foundation

In the past, everything a person knew came from one of only a small number of sources. As a young child, information was provided by parents and extended relatives, neighbours, and in recent years, a finite range of television programming. At school, and via friendship and other social networks, the information provided to children was reasonably uniform. This had advantages and disadvantages, but on the plus side it provided a basic framework for understanding the world, alongside a certain amount of freedom within which to explore, ask questions and learn.

As the person continued to grow, the world began to open further. Firsthand observations, through study, reading for pleasure, film, creative expression, friendships, travel, and other personal experiences merged with expanded observations, through hobbies, interests, and shared experiences with others.

Each person ultimately developed into an adult with a unique sense of self, a unique degree of awareness, education and beliefs, but within a foundational system that was not unique. While factors such as disability, geography, and family dynamics may have contributed to individual isolation, the broader societal framework remained largely uniform. This continuity reinforced the collective nature that defines a society.

When the internet first entered mainstream society, it was heralded as a revolutionary tool destined to unite humanity like never before. People envisioned a borderless world where communication barriers would crumble, enabling instant connections across continents. The web promised to amplify voices, democratize information, and foster understanding between cultures. It was seen as the ultimate equalizer, where everyone, from experts to everyday individuals, could share ideas and collaborate for the greater good. This belief in a digital utopia offered hope for a global village, where technology would bridge distances and dissolve divisions, creating an unprecedented era of unity and progress.

In some ways, the dream of a utopian equalizer has indeed come true. In other ways, it has taken the US and other Western nations down a corrosive path.

While the internet initially promised unity, its open nature also gave rise to significant challenges. By granting a platform to all voices, the digital landscape became an environment where misinformation could easily thrive. This equalization of informed and uninformed opinions meant that credible sources often had to compete with misleading or outright false narratives. Opportunistic actors, both individuals and organizations, have taken advantage of this dynamic, spreading misinformation to serve their agendas. In doing so, they've exploited the internet's reach to amplify harmful ideas, eroding trust in reliable institutions and sowing confusion.

Adding to this complexity is the internet's ability to create echo chambers. Social media algorithms, tailored to users' preferences, often reinforce existing beliefs, making it easier for misinformation to flourish unchallenged. Inside the information bubbles, silos and echo-chambers, fear and division are stoked as users encounter content that confirms their biases while dismissing or silencing opposing viewpoints. Mischievous or malicious entities have weaponized this phenomenon, polarizing societies and turning online disagreements into real-world conflicts. The very tool once envisioned to foster understanding has, paradoxically, become a battleground for discord.

Moreover, the anonymity of the internet emboldens some to spread divisive content without accountability. Trolls and bad actors manipulate emotions, particularly fear and anger, to fuel outrage and further fragment communities. This has created a climate where trust between individuals and groups diminishes, leaving societies more vulnerable to division. Instead of uniting people, the internet in its current form often exacerbates societal fractures, challenging the optimistic vision that accompanied its early days.

The United States, as the cornerstone of Western democracy, championing ideals of liberty, equality, and free expression. Its tradition of open dialogue and self-analysis positioned it as a global leader, inspiring democracies around the world to adopt similar principles. However, the rise of misinformation and divisive rhetoric has corroded the unity that once defined American society. With the advent of the 24-hour news cycle, Cable News networks have amplified this trend, often prioritizing sensationalism and partisan narratives over objective reporting. In a competitive media landscape, some networks have chosen to cater to ideological audiences, reinforcing biases and deepening societal divisions.

Society is no longer a homogenized framework, in which hundreds of thousands, or millions of people reside in proximity to one another, each unique but within a standardised context. Now, societies are expected, encouraged, and arguably bullied into feeling separated from everything and everyone. Many people are confused about who to believe, where to turn for answers, and what is true.

If unity is the foundation of strength, the growing divisions and isolation within the United States have weakened not only its societal fabric but also its ability to lead as the beacon of democracy for the world. As the guiding force for Western cohesion, the internal fractures of the US jeopardize the shared ideals and stability that global democracies rely upon to thrive.

Fifth-Generational Warfare

Fifth-generation warfare (5GW) is a modern, technology-centred combat strategy. 5GW represents a paradigm shift in conflict. It takes the conflict out of the traditional physical space of direct military engagement, and into the realms of information, perception and technology.

This form of warfare leverages tools like social engineering, misinformation, cyberattack, and artificial intelligence to manipulate narratives and influence public opinion. Unlike previous generations of warfare, 5GW blurs the lines of identity. This makes it difficult to know who is a civilian and who is a combatant. The source and intention of the attack is almost impossible to determine. The purpose of 5GW is to destabilize societies, erode trust in institutions, and reshape perceptions without direct confrontation. The brilliance of 5GW is that it simply allows the target society to destroy itself.

The United States has become a prime target for 5GW. Adversarial nations exploit the US tradition of open dialogue, and its reliance on digital communication. Through misinformation campaigns, cyberattacks, and social engineering, foreign and domestic actors aim to destabilize trust in US institutions, polarize communities, and erode the nation's democratic foundations. Social media platforms and Cable News networks amplify these efforts, creating echo chambers that reinforce biases and spread divisive narratives.

As soon as a person picks an unwavering side on any topic of discussion, whether it be men v. women, rich v. poor, Democrat v. Republican, white v. Black, Christian v. Muslim, or any other polarised issue, they become an unwitting participant in the destruction of their own society. 5GW allows the adversary to sit back and watch the target destroy itself from within.

The most widely known recent example of 5GW is the Russian disinformation campaigns during US elections, the most notable of which was the 2016 Presidential Election. Russia has been linked to extensive disinformation efforts aimed at influencing US election outcomes. The campaigns took advantage of social media platforms to spread divisive content, amplify political polarisation and undermine trust in voting systems. Fake social media accounts disseminated misleading information and fanned the flames of division and distrust. The purpose of the campaign was to destabilise American society and weaken its global leadership.

A lesser-known example of 5GW involves Chinese cyber espionage and propaganda. China has been found to employ these strategies against US government agencies and businesses, to steal sensitive information. Simultaneously, state-sponsored propaganda campaigns continuously aim to shape public opinion and challenge US influence around the world.

The internet and cable news have become critical arenas for 5GW tactics. The internet's vast reach and accessibility allow misinformation to spread rapidly, often amplified by social media algorithms that prioritize sensational or divisive content. Cable news networks, with their 24-hour cycles and ideological leanings, further contribute to this distortion by presenting opinion as fact and reinforcing biases. Together, these platforms create an environment where truth is overshadowed by emotionally charged narratives, programming individuals to view the world through polarized lenses. This manipulation fosters fear, distrust, and division, weakening societal cohesion and making communities more susceptible to external influence. It has eroded trust in institutions and fuelled animosity between differing factions, leaving the nation increasingly fragmented.

The repercussions of this internal discord extend far beyond US borders. As a beacon of democratic values, the stability of American society is integral to the cohesion and strength of the Western world. Yet, the divisions wrought by misinformation and amplified by communication forums have weakened this foundation. The resulting instability reverberates across allies and partners, jeopardizing the shared ideals and cooperation that the West depends on to thrive.

As stated in the prophecy, the US is the foundation that gives strength and stability to the West. There are serious cracks in the foundation, which are actively being destroyed as I write this book. Just as it was foretold. However, long before the domino-effect of technological advancement began to negatively impact the US societal framework, other enemies within were already present. These are discussed as we progress through upcoming chapters.

A Spark in Syria?

Over the years I have questioned whether I am recalling an aspect of this section of the prophecy correctly. I am certain that the prophecy referred to a Middle Eastern conflict and that the area was specific to countries in proximity to the Mediterranean Sea, but for some reason I often want to equate the area principally with Syria. I cannot be certain whether Syria was named in the prophecy, or whether my memory has simply attached itself to the concept of Syria.

The geo-political landscape of the Middle East is complex, and tensions arising within the region are common, constantly evolving, and multi-dimensional in nature. I am also as far from an expert in the dynamics of international conflict as a person can be. These points should be taken into account when considering my contextual understanding of the prophecy's relevance to Middle Eastern conflict.

Since the start of 2001, I have become aware of several conflicts near the Mediterranean Sea, in which the United States has had some degree of involvement. The most notable, from the perspective of my understanding of the prophecy, are summarised as follows:

Second Intifada

This conflict began in 2000, which is before the specific parameters of the prophecy. However, it continued until 2005 which is why I have included it. The conflict involved prolonged clashes Israel and Palestine and took place in both territories. US involvement included steady arms sales and diplomatic backing for Israel and engaging in mediation efforts. The US did not directly deploy combat troops to the region. The

US Presidents at the time were Bill Clinton (2000) and George W. Bush (2001 till end of war).

Iraq War

A US-led invasion in 2003 that toppled Saddam Hussein's regime in Iraq, this conflict was followed by prolonged insurgency until 2011, and intense political upheaval. As initiator, the US deployed direct military intervention and extensive troop deployments, airstrikes, and provided large-scale funding for reconstruction efforts. The US Presidents at the time were George W. Bush (2003-2008) and Barack Obama (2009 till end of war).

Lebanon War

This conflict took place over 34 days, from July to August 2006, and between Israel and Hezbollah at the border region between Israel and Lebanon. Hezbollah positioned itself as a defender of Lebanon's Shia Muslim community. However, its actions and allegiances are distinct from those of the official Lebanese government and armed forces and the conflicts involving Hezbollah are decades long. The US provided intelligence sharing, rapid diplomatic consultations and robust arms support for Israel. No direct US ground forces were deployed to intervene in this conflict. The US President at the time was George W. Bush.

Operation Cast Lead

Between December 2008 and January 2009, Israel conducted a major military operation against Hamas on the Gaza Strip, to counter persistent rocket fire and militant infrastructure that had been growing since around 2007. The action sparked widespread international debate. During this event the US maintained strong diplomatic backing for Israel through established channels of arms sales and intelligence sharing, but did not deploy any US troops. The US President at the time was George W. Bush.

Syrian Civil War

This conflict has been ongoing since 2011. It involves a multifaction civil war ignited by the Arab Spring and marked by deep divisions and extensive foreign involvement. It has resulted in a complex humanitarian crisis. During the conflict, the US has engaged covert operations, deployed special forces, overtly supported groups opposing ISIS, and conducted targeted airstrikes against ISIS in Syria, most notably in 2014 and 2017. The US Presidents during this conflict have been Barack Obama (2009-2016), Donald Trump (2017-2020), Joe Biden (2021-2024), and Donald Trump (2025 to present).

Operation Pillar of Defence

In November 2012, Israel activated a sharply focused escalation in response to rocket fire against Israel, primarily from Hamas and to a lesser extent, Palestinian Islamic Jihad. The operation targeted the military infrastructure of these groups to degrade their ability to launch rockets into Israeli territory and to restore security along the border. The US provided diplomatic support, maintained existing arms and intelligence-sharing channels, but did not deploy US troops to the region. The US President during this conflict was Barack Obama.

Gaza-Israel Conflict

A brief but intense flare up of mutual fire occurred in May 2021. Israel was primarily opposing Hamas and Palestinian Islamic Jihad. The militant groups launched a significant number of rockets into Israeli territory, prompting Israel to respond with airstrikes targeting their military infrastructure in the Gaza Strip. The US maintained strong diplomatic backing for Israel, reinforced through arms and intelligence support, and no US ground combat forces were deployed. The US President during this conflict was Joe Biden.

Israel-Hamas War

In October 2023 Hamas carried out a surprise offensive against Israel. The attack sparked a large-scale retaliatory conflict which is still in effect at the time of writing this book. The conflict has primarily been taking place in and around Gaza, and has resulted in widespread devastation of infrastructure, and humanitarian crisis among Palestinian residents in the Gaza region. Throughout this period, the US has provided robust diplomatic, arms, and intelligence support for Israel, despite world-wide criticism and debate about Israel's "heavy-handed" response and the severe impact on the residents of Gaza.

As of the time of writing the US has not deployed ground troops. However, its stance has shifted significantly since the 2024 election. In a joint media event in February 2025, the Presidents of Israel and the US publicly announced plans for the US to "take over" and "own" the Gaza Strip, relocating its Palestinian residents to "wealthy neighbouring countries" and transforming the area into the "Riviera of the Middle East." Despite the unusual nature of this statement, such a strategy would only be viable if US troops were deployed to the region. The US Presidents during this conflict were Joe Biden (2001-2024) and Donald Trump (2025 to present).

In its entirety, this section of the prophecy relates to a double attack on the European democratic nations. The first attack comprises a weakening of the United States. The second attack involves a prolonged or intense conflict that escalates and expands through Europe.

Although it has not received as much media attention as other conflicts in the region, the Syrian Civil War has captured my interest in relation to the prophecy. Its alignment with various aspects of the prophecy is striking and will be explored in greater depth in a future chapter.

Chapter Six
One Man's Stand

> *Amid steady decay of the United States, many will arrive with the idea of supporting themselves, but one man will reverse his retirement and arrive to support others. He will attempt to reverse the outcome of events.*

The prophecy provides a clear dividing line between the response by most people, and the response by a single, outlier individual. The outlier is referred to as a male person specifically; a man who comes out of retirement for the purpose of helping others, rather than to help himself. It is also clear from the prophecy that during this period, a process of "decay" is unfolding, which I discuss later in this chapter.

It is impossible to identify all instances wherein a man, relevant to a process of decay, may have reversed his retirement to help others. At the time of writing this I am aware of various men who have been appointed by sections of the US Government to conduct studies, investigate, litigate, etc. Perhaps one or some of these men are relevant to the prophecy in their own way, and for a particular point in time. I am also aware of men who have, since the turn of the millennium, reversed their retirement due to their concerns about the trajectory of the US in some way. Following are notable examples which are in no way a conclusive list. They are examples that meet the criteria of linking the individual to a period wherein the President of the United States had 5 letters in his last name, and at a time of perceived "decay".

Obama Administration (2008-2015)
David Petraeus (2011-2012)

In 2011, President Barack Obama asked retired General David Petraeus to come out of retirement and serve as the Director of the Central Intelligence Agency (CIA). This decision was driven by the complex and evolving security landscape, particularly the ongoing conflicts in Iraq and Afghanistan, where Petraeus had previously demonstrated exceptional leadership and strategic acumen. The Obama administration faced significant challenges in counterinsurgency and asymmetric warfare, and Petraeus's expertise was seen as crucial in navigating these issues. His appointment aimed to leverage his deep understanding of military strategy and intelligence operations to enhance the effectiveness of US intelligence efforts during a period marked by heightened global threats and the need for experienced leadership.

Originally, Petraeus's appointment was hailed as a masterstroke that leveraged his formidable military background and counterinsurgency expertise to enhance US intelligence amid a period of intricate global challenges. His leadership was expected to recalibrate intelligence operations and sharpen the nation's response to asymmetric warfare.

However, an unforeseen scandal soon derailed this promising trajectory. Revelations emerged that Petraeus had engaged in an extramarital affair with his biographer, Paula Broadwell, which directly resulted in critical breaches of security protocols. The FBI uncovered evidence of the relationship after receiving alerts that Broadwell might have accessed his personal email account. This use of unsecured, personal communication channels to exchange sensitive information posed severe national security risks.

Given his pivotal role as CIA director, these security lapses were deemed intolerable. The scandal compromised Petraeus, calling his judgement and trustworthiness into question. He was forced to resign in November 2012.

The cause for concern that led to Petraeus's appointment was the "decay" of intelligence operations. The "others" that Petraeus was appointed to help were the US intelligence community and the wider US citizenry. The outcome was scandal, and resignation from his position.

Trump administration (2017-2020)
James Mattis (2017-2018)

In 2017, President Donald Trump appointed retired General James Mattis as Secretary of Defence, marking a significant return to public service for the highly respected military leader. Mattis, who had retired from active military service in 2013, was known for his strategic acumen and principled leadership. His appointment came at a time when the United States faced evolving global threats, including terrorism and strategic rivalries with nations such as Russia and China. The decision to bring Mattis out of retirement was driven by a need for experienced and steady leadership in navigating these complex national security challenges.

Mattis played a key role in shaping US defence strategy, emphasizing the importance of alliances and partnerships, and advocating for a strong and capable military. However, his tenure was also characterized by tensions with the Trump administration, particularly over issues such as the US withdrawal from the Iran nuclear deal and the handling of relations with NATO allies. These disagreements ultimately led to Mattis's resignation in December 2018, citing differences in policy and vision.

The cause for concern that led to Mattis's appointment was the "decay" arising from a rise in terrorism and strategic rivalries. The "others" that Mattis was appointed to help were the US military and the wider US citizenry. The outcome was resignation based on irreconcilable differences.

Robert Mueller (2017-2019)

Robert Mueller was a former FBI Director who had retired from public service. In 2017 he was appointed as Special Counsel to oversee the investigation into Russian interference in the 2016 US presidential election. Deputy Attorney General Rod Rosenstein appointed Mueller amid growing concerns about potential collusion between the Trump presidential campaign and Russian operatives. Broader issues of election integrity and foreign influence on American democracy were also concerns at the time. Mueller's extensive background in law enforcement and his reputation for impartiality and thoroughness made him a fitting choice to lead such a high-stakes investigation.

The outcome of Mueller's investigation was multifaceted. His team produced a detailed report in 2019, which concluded that while there was insufficient evidence to charge members of the Trump campaign with conspiring with Russia, there were numerous instances of potential obstruction of justice by President Trump. The report also highlighted the extensive efforts by Russian entities to interfere in the election. The findings led to significant political and public debate, with accusations on both sides of bias, witch-hunt and coverup. A notable feature of the outcome at the time was the rebranding of the report by Trump's US Attorney, William Barr, which was viewed by many to be a whitewashing of the report's findings on Trump. It later also transpired that the remit of the Mueller investigative team had been limited to non-financial investigations only. This prevented access to financial records that may have demonstrated motive or transactional relationships.

The cause for concern that led to Mueller's appointment was the "decay" of US sovereignty due to interference and collusion with foreign adversarial nations. The "others" that Mueller was appointed to help were the wider US citizenry by protecting the integrity of the US electoral process, upholding the rule of law, and ensuring that any potential wrongdoing by public officials was thoroughly examined. The outcome was indictments against 34 individuals and 3 companies, 8 guilty pleas, and a conviction at trial. However, the central figure of the investigation, Donald Trump remained largely unaffected.

Biden administration (2021-2024)

Joe Biden (campaign and presidency 2020-2024)

In 2020, Joe Biden, who had stepped back from active political roles after serving as Vice President from 2009 to 2017, decided to run for President of the United States. His decision to come out of retirement was driven by his deep concerns about the country's trajectory, particularly in terms of political polarization, social justice, and the handling of the COVID-19 pandemic. Biden's campaign emphasized the need to restore the "soul of America," address systemic inequalities, and navigate the country through the health crisis.

The outcome of Biden's presidency included significant policy initiatives to directly address the issues that motivated his return to public service. His administration focused on tackling the COVID-19 pandemic through widespread vaccination efforts, economic relief packages, and measures to support public health. Biden also prioritised policies aimed at racial justice, economic equity, and climate change. However, his presidency faced a torrent of political opposition, and a wide-spread media campaign designed to undermine his achievements and raise suspicions about his mental health, adherence to law, private and professional affiliations, and financial relationships. Ultimately, Biden was challenged by his own political party, amid calls for him to step down due to advanced age and unproved allegations of deteriorating mental health. After resisting these calls, he ultimately yielded on the condition that his Vice President, Kamala Harris take his place as Presidential Candidate for the Democratic Party.

The cause for concern that led to Biden's presidency was the "decay" in the "soul of America", comprising of health, corruption, social and economic equities, and fractured foreign relationships. The "others" that Biden wanted to help related to the US citizenry and Western alliance partners. The outcome was forfeiture of a second term as President.

John Kerry (2021-2024)

In 2021, John Kerry, who had retired from public office after serving as Secretary of State from 2013 to 2017, was appointed as the Special Presidential Envoy for Climate by President Joe Biden. Kerry's return to public service was driven by a deep concern for climate change and the urgent need for the United States to take a leading role in addressing global environmental challenges. His appointment came at a time when the world was grappling with the escalating impacts of climate change, and there was a growing recognition of the need for coordinated international action to mitigate its effects. Kerry's extensive experience in diplomacy and his long-standing commitment to environmental issues made him a fitting choice to spearhead the US efforts in this critical area.

The outcome of Kerry's tenure as Special Presidential Envoy for Climate resulted in a temporary re-engagement of the United States in global climate initiatives. President Trump had withdrawn the US from the Paris Agreement in 2017, and Kerry played a key role in the US rejoining the Agreement in February 2021. He resigned from the role in March 2024 citing that "Congress is frozen", along with a desire to assist with the Biden Presidential campaign. Within hours of re-taking office in January 2025 President Trump signed an executive order to withdraw the US from the Paris Agreement once again.

The cause for concern that led to Kerry's appointment was the "decay" in the US leadership response to climate and environmental issues. The "others" that Kerry wanted to help related to the US citizenry and the international community. The outcome was short term success, which was later overturned.

Trump administration (2025)

I am writing this book in early to mid-2025, shortly after the commencement of Donald Trump's second term as US President. It is too early to identify any men who may be of significance to the prophecy. However, it will be easy to spot them. As time progresses, there may be opportunities to examine further examples of men who potentially fulfil the requirements of the prophecy.

The examples provided herein demonstrate that the prophecy's use of the term "decay" could be applied to a single topic, or a multitude of different topics. The COVID-19 pandemic claimed a staggering 1.1

million lives in the United States. The rate of COVID-19 deaths per capita was unusually high considering the US leading the world in Gross Domestic Product (GDP) and Human Development Index (HDI). The decay in this regard could be interpreted as a decay in health and mortality rates, or the management of these things.

Similarly, political tensions, economic inequities and societal unrest could be interpreted as a decay in the domestic condition of the United States. A breakdown in military competency, national security, state sovereignty and foreign relations could all be interpreted as a decay in the international standing of the United States. The world of domestic and international complexities to which the term "decay" of the US may relate to are beyond the reach of this book.

Suffice to say that each of the individuals noted above may be relevant to the prophecy. Each of them reversed his retirement to focus on an area or areas of concern involving perceived "decay" relevant to the US. Each of them was a notable reversal of retirement during the presidency of a man with 5 letters to his last name.

The Steady Decay

Reference is made to a "steady decay of the United States". Countries can experience various forms of "decay" over time. Internal and external factors may exist separately or may combine to compound upon each other. Examples of decay that could apply to the US include:

Political Decay

Political decay refers to the gradual weakening of a nation's political systems, institutions, and governance. It often manifests as increased polarization, where opposing political factions become so divided that collaboration becomes nearly impossible. This gridlock can erode the government's ability to address pressing issues effectively. Additionally, when trust in institutions like the judiciary or electoral systems diminishes, citizens may lose faith in the very structures meant to uphold democracy and fairness.

Corruption or authoritarian tendencies can further accelerate political decay, as leaders prioritize personal or partisan interests over the public good. Over time, these factors can destabilize a nation's political foundation, making it vulnerable to internal unrest or external manipulation. In essence, political decay undermines the principles of accountability, transparency, and unity that are essential for a thriving democracy.

Similar political challenges presently appear in the US. Examples include legislative gridlock in Congress, where partisan divisions have delayed or blocked critical legislation, such as funding bills. Concerns about democratic erosion have also been raised, with reports highlighting actions perceived as undermining institutional checks and balances. The result has been an ever-increasing difficulty to maintain effective governance and public trust.

Economic Decay

The concept of economic decay encompasses a range of factors that can erode a nation's financial stability and prosperity over time. For the United States, various challenges have emerged that highlight vulnerabilities within its economic framework. From shifts in global competitiveness to growing disparities in wealth distribution, these issues paint a complex picture of a nation grappling with internal and external pressures. Below are some notable examples that illustrate how these dynamics are manifesting in contemporary America.

The US has faced challenges in maintaining its global economic edge, with concerns about the impact of trade wars and tariff policies. For instance, recent tariffs have strained trade relationships with key partners like China, Mexico, and Canada, contributing to market volatility and fears of a potential recession.

Economic disparities continue to grow, with wealth increasingly concentrated among the top earners. This has led to social and economic tensions, as highlighted in various reports on the widening gap between the rich and the poor.

Cities like Detroit, Michigan, and Gary, Indiana, have struggled with the aftermath of industrial decline. These areas face high unemployment, crumbling infrastructure, and stagnant economic growth, reflecting broader challenges in revitalizing once-thriving regions.

Social and Cultural Decay

Societal and cultural decay refers to the gradual erosion of shared values, social cohesion, and cultural identity within a society. This can manifest as weakening trust in institutions, increasing divisions among communities, and the loss of moral or ethical standards. It often leads to fragmentation, where individuals prioritize self-interest over collective well-being, and traditional frameworks that once provided stability begin to deteriorate.

In the United States a combination of society-based erosions is evident. Rising polarization and divisive rhetoric have contributed to a fragmented society, with communities becoming increasingly isolated along ideological lines. Social media and entertainment have turned popular culture towards the routine glorification of materialism and self-interest, resulting in a decline in moral and ethical standards. Whereas previously a religious deity might be worshipped, now a similar style of adulation can be given to dissenting voices, algorithmic online content, and artificially generated personalities. In one notable example, a well-known current affairs program recently explored the rise of artificial intelligence companions and the emotional connections people form with them. The episode delved into the phenomenon of individuals falling in love with their AI partners, including a woman who reportedly married her AI companion!

In striking contrast to moral decline, fundamentalism is also on the rise. Fundamentalism, particularly when it becomes rigid or intolerant, can contribute to societal decay by fostering divisions between groups with differing beliefs. For instance, in the US, the rise of certain fundamentalist movements has been linked to increased polarization and challenges to pluralism. These movements often resist modernity and promote strict adherence to specific ideologies, which can exacerbate cultural divides and hinder social cohesion. It is likely that both the decline in morals and ethics, plus the rise in fundamentalism, are direct reactions to one another – further evidencing the extreme polarizations within.

Another aspect of societal decay appears as a loss of trust in the country's institutions. Public confidence in government, media and other key institutions in the US has declined significantly since the 1960s, influenced by events such as the Vietnam War and the Watergate scandal in the 1970s. For example, public trust in the federal government was at its highest in 1964, with about 77% of Americans expressing trust in the government to do what is right "just about always" or "most of the time." However, this trust has steadily declined over the decades, reaching one of its lowest points in 2023, with only 16% of Americans expressing similar trust.

Other Forms of Decay

Of the remaining forms of decay that a country can experience, which may apply to the United States, *global influence decay* is the most relevant to the prophecy. Global influence decay is a reduction of geopolitical influence in comparison to other rising powers, or as alliances with other nations begin to weaken. Loss of perceived credibility on the global stage can also contribute to global influence decay, if a country exhibits inconsistent or isolationist foreign policies.

The United States has yo-yoed in this respect, depending on the president in power. However, overall, the US is perceived to have a diminished global influence, the relevance of which is covered later in this book.

Neglect of critical infrastructure, such as roads, bridges and public utilities is a form of infrastructure decay. Similarly, failing to keep pace with technological advancements can cause divide between a country and other countries that are more advanced.

Finally, environmental decay can occur through over-exploitation of natural resources, or a lack of climate action. Each of these areas of decay are visible in the United States in recent years. However, the prophecy specifically refers to a foundational decay which I have come to believe refers to internal factors such as politics, economy and societal interactions.

It seems to me that the "foundation" of the United States as leader of the West relates to its political, economic and societal strengths. For this reason, I have decided to focus my examination on these internal forms of decay, as being most aligned to the prophecy.

It is sufficient to conclude with an acknowledgment that every form of decay which is present in a country can compound the others, creating a cycle that may be difficult to reverse.

Ancient Examples of Internal Decay

Many an ancient empire has fallen at the hands of gradual internal, foundational decay.

Mayan Civilization (2000 BC – 1600 AD approx.)

The Mayans suffered a foundational decay of their civilization largely due to deep political divisions and persistent warfare among its many city-states, which undermined overall stability. Furthermore, environmental mismanagement, including deforestation and overuse of resources during a time of limited global commerce, contributed to agricultural decline and societal stress, eventually accelerating the civilization's collapse.

Han Dynasty of China (200 BC – 220 AD approx.)

In the Han Dynasty internal decay was driven by political rivalry and divisions within the ruling elite, which gradually weakened central authority. Corruption became rampant, with factions such as influential eunuchs manipulating power to their advantage. These factors destabilized the government and contributed to the dynasty's downfall.

Roman Empire (27 BC – 476 AD approx.)

The Roman Empire experienced significant internal decay characterized by political instability and ineffective leadership. Corruption permeated the system, and constant power struggles often led to the assassination or overthrow of emperors. These internal crises, combined with external pressures, hastened the empire's decline.

Modern Examples of Internal Decay

Similar examples of weakening and internal decay can be found in the modern world of leadership. The following are some of the most notable examples, however even more recent societal downfalls can be found in smaller scale around the world.

Ottoman Empire (1299-1922)

The Ottoman Empire faced significant internal decay in its later centuries, with corruption and administrative inefficiency undermining its governance. Power struggles among the ruling elite often led to instability, while nepotism and favouritism weakened the effectiveness of leadership. Additionally, as the empire expanded, managing vast territories became increasingly complex, leading to difficulties in maintaining order and unity. These internal challenges, combined with external pressures from rising European powers, ultimately contributed to the empire's decline and eventual dissolution.

British Empire (1583-1997)

It seems unnatural to consider the United Kingdom an "empire" these days. The countries collectively referred to as "Britain" are allied cousins to all other countries of the West. But Britain was indeed an empire, and the attributes that contributed to its empire status continued until around the end of the last millennium. For this reason, I shall adhere to the empire description to illustrate the points I wish to make.

The British Empire was once the largest empire in history, spanning continents and influencing global politics, economics, and culture. However, its decline was marked by significant internal decay, which became increasingly evident in the 1900s. Economic challenges played a major role, as the financial strain of maintaining such a vast empire, particularly after World Wars One and Two, left Britain in a weakened position. The cost of war efforts drained resources, and the empire struggled to recover economically, leading to questions about the viability of its global dominance.

Political divisions within Britain and its colonies further accelerated the empire's decline. The rise of nationalist movements in colonies like India, Kenya, and Malaya highlighted growing discontent with British rule. These movements, often fuelled by demands for self-determination and resistance to colonial exploitation, gained momentum in the mid-1900s. Leaders like Mahatma Gandhi and Jomo Kenyatta became symbols of resistance, forcing Britain to confront the unsustainability of its imperial ambitions.

Additionally, the empire's administrative inefficiency and reliance on outdated systems of governance made it increasingly difficult to manage its vast territories. The decolonization process, which began in earnest after World War Two, saw over 60 countries gain independence, culminating in the handover of Hong Kong to China in 1997.

The fall of the British Empire profoundly reshaped Britain's national identity, economy, and societal structure. Economically, the loss of colonies curtailed access to valuable resources and markets, disrupting industries once reliant on imperial trade and contributing to Britain's declining global influence. Culturally, it prompted a national reckoning, fuelling both nostalgia and deeper reflection on Britain's evolving place in the world. Immigration from former colonies enriched British society with diversity, sparking debates about integration and identity.

Despite these debates, British society has largely embraced its multicultural diversity. I recall traveling to Britain for the Year 2000 celebrations after living in the United States for several years. One immediate difference I noticed was the way people interacted across ethnic lines.

A particularly memorable moment occurred while dining with a relative at a restaurant. In Atlanta, where I had lived for years, it was extremely rare to see a Black man and a white woman as a couple, especially in public spaces or mainstream media. This dynamic has certainly changed over time, though I can't speak to current perceptions. Twenty-five years ago, such relationships were scarcely depicted in television shows, movies, or commercials. Occasionally, the pairing appeared in reverse - a white man with a Black woman - but even that was uncommon.

When a mixed-race couple entered the restaurant that evening in Britain, I instinctively noticed them. What struck me most, however, was that no one else seemed to register their presence. This realization sparked an inner shift, one that eventually led me to migrate to Britain where I lived for 15 years. It wasn't a deliberate decision based solely on that moment, but the lingering thoughts it provoked - about diversity, social norms, and personal perception - continued to shape my curiosity until I decided to move.

For the record, I thoroughly enjoyed my years in Britain, just as I did in the United States, and as I do now in Australia. Every country has its own set of strengths, and I deeply appreciate how no two nations are alike, even when they share surface-level similarities.

Ultimately, this fleeting moment in time reveals much about people, society, and the broader evolution of social norms. More importantly, it underscores a critical truth: the decline of a nation's imperial dominance does not equate to its demise. It simply marks the end of an era, not the end of the nation itself.

Finally, when it comes to its political standing in the world, Britain, for which the correct name is the United Kingdom, incorporating England, Wales, Scotland and Northern Ireland, has adopted a middle power role in the world, focusing on alliances like NATO to maintain influence. The British Empire, which excludes Northern Ireland, has enduring cultural legacy around the world. Australia and New Zealand are no longer British colonies, but other country continue to be. The term has been changed however to "British Overseas Territories", and the 14 countries that fall within the British territories enjoy varying degrees of self-governance.

Soviet Union (1922-1991)

Soviet Russia experienced a prolonged period of internal decay that ultimately led to its dissolution. Political rivalry within the Communist Party became increasingly pronounced over time, as factions vied for control, leading to inconsistent policies and weakened central authority. This infighting created an environment of distrust and inefficiency within the government, which hindered its ability to address the nation's growing challenges. Corruption was rampant, with officials often prioritizing their own interests over the needs of the state.

Economically, the centrally planned system proved unable to sustain growth or adapt to changing global conditions. Industrial inefficiencies, military over-investment, and a shortage of consumer goods led to widespread public dissatisfaction. By the 1980s, the economy was stagnating. Living standards for ordinary citizens had significantly declined. This led to growing unrest and public disillusionment towards the government.

The Soviet leader of the time, Mikhail Gorbachev, attempted a variety of reform policies, including increased "glasnost" (increased transparency), and "perestroika" (restructuring). These changes were aimed as modernizing the political and economic systems of Russia. However, the reforms backfired, causing the government to lose grip on what had previously been tightly held information, which led to an increase in public criticism. Nationalist movements within the Soviet republics, fuelled by decades of suppression and cultural tensions, gained momentum during this time. The combination of political discontent, economic hardship, and the rise of nationalist aspirations culminated in the Soviet Union's collapse in 1991, as republics declared independence and the central government dissolved.

The collapse of the Soviet Union had profound effects on Russia and its people. Economically, it led to a transition from a centrally planned system to a market economy, causing widespread inflation, unemployment, and loss of savings. Politically, Russia emerged as an independent state but struggled with corruption and weak governance during the 1990s. Socially, the collapse created uncertainty and hardship, as many citizens faced declining living standards and a loss of national identity.

Almost 35 years has since passed, and the collapse of the Soviet Union continues to impact Russian people today. Economically, there are lasting inequalities, with wealth concentrated among a small elite while many still face financial struggles. Politically, the loss of superpower status has influenced national identity, with some citizens yearning for the perceived stability of the Soviet era. Socially, the shattering of the Soviet Union disrupted cultural ties and created tensions with neighbouring former republics, most notable of which is Ukraine, impacting regional relations and individual lives. For some in Russia, reclaiming influence over Ukraine is seen as a way to restore the perceived greatness lost with the Soviet Union's dissolution and to counter Western expansion into Eastern Europe.

In some ways, it causes the country to easily fall into a sense of needing to return to its "empire status", which is unlikely to ever be achieved, unless through some form of widescale international conflict, such as a world war. It is for this reason that discerning eyes often regard Russia to be a threat to global world order, a matter closely related to the prophecy as appears evident throughout this book.

Harnessing Decay

The prophecy refers to the "many" who will "arrive with the idea of supporting themselves". Although I cannot conclusively determine what this part of prophecy means, on the face of it the message seems self-explanatory and is likely to fall within two separate categories. The first is a matter of *transformative agenda*, the second is *crisis exploitation*. In some ways these two threads are alike, in other ways they diverge.

Transformative Agenda

Individuals with a transformative agenda often emerge as rallying figures during times of societal decay. Even if their personal record is less than impeccable, the breakdown of societal norms gives them an opportunity to sell an idea of renewal and revitalization to a population desperate for change.

For example, in the aftermath of the 2008 global financial crisis, widespread disillusionment with the established political and economic order paved the way for populist leaders in the United States. The most notable person to harness this opportunity was Donald Trump, who in 2015-16 aligned his vision to the collective frustration of an electorate battered by recession and perceived governmental neglect. Trump promised to dismantle the established elite and restore lost national pride.

A similar dynamic played out in Europe in around the same period. As longstanding political structures struggled to address rapid societal changes and economic disparities, leaders like Marine Le Pen in France and Viktor Orbán in Hungary capitalized on public discontent. They tapped into nationalist sentiments and the nostalgia for a return to perceived better times, positioning themselves as both outsiders and saviours amid an environment of decay. Their rhetoric resonated with voters who felt abandoned by a system no longer working in their favour, even as these leaders sometimes exhibited personal or policy-related shortcomings.

History shows that when the social contract breaks down - whether through corruption, economic mismanagement, or cultural disintegration - charismatic figures exploit the ensuing power vacuum. In moments when the collective faith in governing institutions wanes, even leaders who have significant personal flaws can rise by offering simple, emotionally compelling solutions to complex problems.

As a society steadily declines, its citizens often become more receptive to bold, albeit imperfect, figures who pledge to restore order and rekindle national pride. Their rise to power is less about personal virtue and more about their ability to harness the collective longing for change into a formidable political force. What they offer may not be a true solution, but rather a compelling vision. Yet, if that vision arrives at the right moment, it can be embraced as a solution by a public desperate for something to believe in.

A transformative agenda is strategic and long-term. When effectively implemented, it can reshape society, potentially leading to widespread change, civil unrest, or even international conflict.

Exploiting a Crisis

Crisis exploitation is when individuals or groups insert themselves into emerging crises or tragedies. There may be a variety of reasons for doing so, but 2 notable reasons are to grab attention and monetise the event. Any event that has public attention can attract crisis exploiters. Exploiting a crisis shares some of the qualities of transformative agenda, but it tends to be less strategic, shorter-range, and is often more likely to be limited to individual and group benefit.

The range of crises exploitation can vary tremendously. On the minor scale, a person may simply exaggerate their knowledge and abilities in the hopes of being seen as informative or helpful. On the major scale, groups and individuals may deliberately mislead the public in ways that harm or even kill people. The act of exploiting the crisis serves to divert attention away from what's important and create an illusion that the crisis exploiter is somehow relevant to the circumstances. The opposite is generally true as illustrated by the following examples.

9/11 Terrorist Attacks (2001)

Alicia Esteve Head, a Spanish businesswoman, falsely claimed to be a 9/11 survivor under the name Tania Head, fabricating a story about escaping the South Tower and losing her fiancé in the North Tower. Her deception earned widespread sympathy, leading to her becoming President of the World Trade Center Survivors Network. In 2007, investigations revealed she had never been in the United States during the attacks. After returning to Spain, she was suspected of authoring a false letter claiming she had taken her own life.

Hurricane Katrina (2005)

In the wake of Hurricane Katrina, several opportunists emerged. Some individuals falsely portrayed themselves as heroic first responders or created dubious charity initiatives to solicit donations. Some of the individuals involved were discovered, others were not. Those who were discovered were widely criticized for exploiting the tragedy rather than contributing meaningfully to recovery efforts.

The Cancer Cure Guru (2015)

Belle Gibson was an Australian influencer who rose to prominence in around 2015. Gibson claimed to have cured her terminal brain cancer using natural remedies and a strict diet. This was a story that she widely promoted on social media to market her wellness brand. She caught the attention of Apple Inc., who helped her develop a highly successful app called The Wholefood Pantry. Gibson's narrative resonated with many social media followers who were desperate for hope amid serious health crises. As she rose to fame, Gibson was discovered to have failed to distribute public donations as promised. This led to a wider investigation that ultimately revealed that her cancer diagnosis was fabricated, and that she may have been feigning life-threatening illnesses since her youth.

COVID-19 pandemic (2019)

During the COVID-19 pandemic, some opportunistic figures on social media exploited the crisis by promoting unverified "miracle cures" and conspiracy theories to drive engagement and profits. For example, certain influencers and fraudulent accounts on platforms like Facebook and TikTok pushed dubious supplements and treatment methods, capitalising on public fear and misinformation to monetise clicks and affiliate sales.

Social media has given rise to numerous opportunities to exploit public anxieties for personal or financial gain. No media platform is exempt from this phenomenon. The COVID-19 pandemic and persistent lively debate about Donald Trump's influences on the United States have created a magnificent array of opportunities for exploiters to slip themselves into the story.

An Attempt to Reverse

The remaining aspect of this section of the prophecy that I have found curious is the reference made to the "attempt to reverse" the outcome of events. The phrase seems to suggest that successful reversal is unlikely. Alternatively, the phrase may allow for success or failure, depending on other circumstantial factors.

It is a very small part of the prophecy which seems to suggest that the prophecy will continue to unfold, regardless of how many men come out of retirement, and even if it is forestalled along the way. It is equally possible that the phrase "attempt to reverse" is a deliberately placed clue that serves a purpose.

Chapter Seven
Society Engineered

> *The people will be trained to become like rats.*

This aspect of the prophecy took me some time to decipher. The sentence runs directly after a previous sentence which refers to the United States. The indication therefore is that this sentence refers to the US population. However, the phrase "trained to become like rats" does not fit with the image that comes to mind when a person thinks about the American people.

It is obviously a difficult and delicate task for someone living outside of the United States to attempt to characterise the nation's citizenry, as it relates to "rats". It can seem arrogant and dismissive an act in the eyes of American readers. I have wanted to avoid discussing this aspect of the prophecy for exactly this reason. However, to correctly recount the prophecy, as it was presented to me 4 decades ago, it becomes necessary to recount all of it, rather than skip the parts that are uncomfortable for me to write, or for others to read. I make the best attempt that I can, reminding readers that I did not write the prophecy. I have, however, spent many years trying to accurately interpret it. This is the closest I have been able to achieve, keeping in mind the evolution of an ever-changing societal and political dynamic in the United States since I first discovered the prophecy.

Characterising the American People

Just as any other nationality of people will have their own stereotypes, the American stereotypes consist of positive and negative examples. Words and phrases like "gun obsessed" or "friendly" are commonly used to describe average Americans. The open dialogue that the United States is known for also gives rise to other stereotypes, such as "arrogant", "racist", "patriotic", and "generous".

Rats, on the other hand, are generally considered to be dirty, carrying infection, or scavenging in hidden placed, over-breeding. None of these characteristics or stereotypes are akin to being American. It just did not make sense, so instead I focused on what Americans are generally known for. This sentence in the prophecy was the shortest, but it took years for me to decipher. And this can be seen by the length to which I must explain how I deciphered a comparatively small part of the prophecy.

The United States is known for publicly airing its dirty laundry, an approach many perceive as arrogance or self-indulgence. I disagree. Transparency, however uncomfortable, holds undeniable value.

I live in a country where most of its Indigenous people are economically confined to the northern reaches, enduring relentless heat, barren landscapes, and an overwhelming presence of flies - a reality difficult to grasp without firsthand experience. Their access to education, employment, and upward mobility remains severely limited.

Despite gradual improvements in integration since the 1980s, Indigenous Australians still face substantial barriers compared to their counterparts in the United States and New Zealand. The US recognizes Native American tribes as sovereign nations, allowing them to govern themselves within federal law. While Indigenous communities face economic and social challenges and are still impacted by historical injustices – such as forced removals and broken treaties - they have legal protections, land rights, and access to federal programs.

New Zealand has a formal treaty with its Indigenous Māori population - the *Treaty of Waitangi (1840)* - which has provided a legal framework for Indigenous rights and land claims. Māori culture is widely integrated into national identity, with language revitalization efforts, political representation, and economic partnerships which, despite their imperfections, help to strengthen Indigenous inclusion.

Even relative to the United Kingdom's integration of Black and white citizenry, Australia lags. And yet, few open discussions acknowledge this slow-moving effort.

In 2017, leaders for Indigenous Australians issued a reform proposal at the First Nations National Constitutional Convention. *The Uluru Statement from the Heart* was a document calling for constitutional recognition of Indigenous Australians. It proposed three key reforms: a voice, a treaty, and the truth.

In 2023, Australia held a referendum to determine whether Indigenous Australians should have a constitutional right to representation, allowing them to make formal proposals to Federal Parliament. They were simply asking for a voice, the first of the 3 key reforms outlined in the Uluru Statement proposal. The Australian Indigenous Voice Referendum, held on 14 October 2023, was rejected by over 60% of voters and failed to pass in any state. Most Australians opted not to hear Indigenous voices. It seems they preferred the comfort of silence over the uncomfortable confrontation of reality. As any reader might have guessed – I enthusiastically voted **YES**.

As someone who loves Australia but has gained perspective from living abroad, I can't help but wonder how openly confronting our societal shortcomings - rather than preserving dignified silence - might bring about meaningful change. Perhaps more airing of dirty laundry could be exactly what's needed.

Notwithstanding my admiration for open dialogue, America's culture of openness, despite benefiting those who are marginalised, also raises an intriguing question. In a nation where confrontation is constant, where self-examination is routine, is there a deeper, unintended effect at play? Could this relentless transparency train Americans toward a particular characteristic - one eerily linked to rats?

But what characteristic would that be?

Rights and Freedoms

The rights and freedoms afforded by the United States Constitution, give every American a right to be heard that is unparalleled across the world. The following is a comparison of overall rights and freedoms of the US population against other nations that rank highest in speech protections. To begin, nations are referenced in descending order of strength of speech protection.

United States

The First Amendment provides extensive protection for free speech, allowing a wide range of expression without fear of government censorship. It allows for fewer restrictions compared to many other countries, with only a few exceptions including speech that incites violence, defamation, and certain obscenities.

Canada

The Canadian Charter of Rights and Freedoms guarantees freedom of expression but includes reasonable limits to balance other rights and societal values. For example, hate speech and speech that incites violence are restricted.

United Kingdom

The UK protects free speech under common law and the Human Rights Act of 1998. However, it has specific laws against hate speech, defamation, and speech that threatens public order or national security.

Germany

The Grundgesetz, which translates to "The German Basic Law" ensures freedom of expression but includes restrictions on speech that incites hatred, violence, or discriminates against individuals, particularly in the context of the country's history.

Australia

While Australia does not have a Bill of Rights, the High Court of Australia recognizes an implied right to freedom of political communication. Nevertheless, free speech is balanced with other legal restrictions, such as defamation laws and anti-discrimination legislation.

Every Man for Himself

There is another comparison to be made between the United States and other countries afforded strong speech protections, which I believe aligns the American people to a type of "training". This comparison relates to the degree to which a nation's population is supported by socialist or "safety net" policies.

In this context, let's view those same 5 countries again, as they rank in descending order of people protections relating to common needs, specifically social benefits, workers' rights, access to healthcare, and education.

Germany

Germany enjoys the highest place in this regard, with one of the most comprehensive *social benefits* systems in the world, including health and accident insurance, worker's and employees' benefits, pensions, and miner' insurance. Strong labor laws protect *workers' rights*, including generous paid leave, parental leave, and unemployment benefits. Germany's *healthcare* system is highly regarded, with compulsory health insurance covering nearly all residents. Germany offers free or low-cost *education*, including higher education, with a strong emphasis on vocational training.

Canada

Canada provides a range of *social benefits*, including unemployment insurance, child benefits, and old-age security. Canadian labor laws ensure *workers' rights*, including paid leave, parental leave, and protections against unfair dismissal. Canada has a publicly funded *healthcare* system that provides universal coverage for medically necessary services. *Education* is publicly funded and accessible, with dedicated support for both primary and secondary education.

United Kingdom

The UK has a well-established *social benefits* system, including unemployment benefits, child benefits, and pensions. UK labor laws protect *workers' rights*, including paid leave, parental leave, and protections against unfair dismissal. The National Health Service (NHS) provides universal *healthcare* coverage, funded through taxation. *Education* is publicly funded and accessible, with dedicated support for primary and secondary education.

Australia

Australia offers a range of *social benefits*, including unemployment benefits, child benefits, and pensions. Australian labor laws protect *workers' rights*, including paid leave, parental leave, and protections against unfair dismissal. Australia's *healthcare* system, Medicare, provides universal coverage for medically necessary services. *Education* is publicly funded and accessible, with dedicated support for primary and secondary education.

United States

The US has a less comprehensive *social benefits* system compared to the other countries, with limited unemployment benefits, child benefits, and pensions. US labor laws provide fewer *workers' rights*, with limited paid leave and parental leave. The US *healthcare* system is primarily privatized, with significant disparities in access and affordability. *Education* is publicly funded and accessible, but there are significant disparities in quality and access, particularly in higher education.

Normalization of Abuse

I recently connected with a woman who happened to be a member of my audience. She reached out via email to express her appreciation for a series of episodes I was developing on Gnosticism, an early Christian belief system that placed greater emphasis on the Feminine aspect of the Divine than the Abrahamic traditions typically do. Intrigued by her background, I explored her website and discovered that she was an author focused on Goddess Spirituality - a movement that emerged in the 1960s, centered on feminine influence, empowerment, and humanity's connection to nature.

That woman was Rev. Dr. Karen Tate, a multi-disciplinary spiritualist and social justice activist. One of her books, *Normalizing Abuse: A Commentary on the Culture of Pervasive Abuse* (2024), immediately caught my attention. In it, Tate examines how patriarchal systems, reinforced by institutional norms, perpetuate cycles of abuse in everyday life. While her analysis presents a broad societal critique, it is deeply rooted in personal experience, making her insights both profound and relatable. Her journey led her to explore how the normalization of abuse infiltrates American daily life, shaping perceptions and influencing behavior in ways many fail to recognize.

The routine acceptance of pervasive abuse is embedded in American culture. Hyper-partisan political dialogue compels voters to commit unwavering loyalty to one of the dominant parties, even when doing so contradicts their own best interests. Within religious traditions, doctrines of sin and guilt push worshippers toward self-denial and self-punishment as acts of devotion. Meanwhile, sex and sexualization are wielded both as instruments of power, success, and achievement, and as weapons of shame, guilt, and control.

Pervasive abuse manifests in nearly every facet of daily life - academia, law enforcement, the military, the workplace, media, religion, government, culture, family dynamics, and personal relationships. Combined with the absence of robust safety nets, the level of stress that ordinary Americans endure is extraordinary.

Among the many divisive cultural debates shaping American society, immigration policy stands for me, out as one of the most emotionally charged. Though just one of many ongoing societal conflicts, it affects vast numbers of people, warranting particular attention.

According to the most recent Census data, approximately 21% of couple-led households in the US include at least one foreign-born spouse. Additionally, around 25% of the US population consists of foreign-born individuals or first-generation Americans - those with at least one immigrant parent.

While these figures overlap in some cases, a reasonable estimate suggests that over 40% of US households have a direct connection to immigration, whether through a foreign-born spouse or first-generation American family members. Ongoing public threats of family separations, deportations of undocumented migrants, and revocations of citizenship status mean that nearly half of US households either face direct risks from drastic immigration policy shifts or have a close family member who does.

Yet, the debate rages on. I remember it raging when I lived in the US during the 1990s. And it continues today, never reaching a definitive resolution. It simply persists, along with the many other polarizing topics that pervade American households and consciousness on a daily basis.

And then there is the ongoing debate about guns, which almost every person living outside of the United States instinctively shakes their head at in dismay. Gun rights and school shootings – the quintessential Americanism that infinitely rages on.

What is the impact of such a uniquely American level of stress on the US population?

Life Expectancy

Americans may lead in free speech protections, yet among the same group of countries, their ranking falls to the lowest when it comes to safeguards that directly impact daily life. However, this decline is not sufficient to establish a direct link between U.S. protections and the prophecy.

To further explore this, I examined life expectancy data relative to the same five countries. Factors influencing life expectancy - such as lifestyle, environment, and socioeconomics – vary across nations, complicating comparisons and requiring careful consideration.

Australia

The overall life expectancy of Australians is 84.18 years, which is highest among the five countries. Men average 81.1 years, and women average 85.1 years.

Canada

Ranking second overall is Canada with a population overall life expectancy of 83.26 years. Men tend to live an average of 79.5 years, and women average lifespan is 83.9 years.

United Kingdom

British men average life expectancy is 78.6 years, and women average 82.6 years. Overall life expectancy is 82.06 years.

Germany

The overall life expectancy of the German population is 82.2 years, with women living an average of 83 years, and men averaging 78.2 years.

United States

While the comparison reveals small variations across all countries, the United States ranks lowest in overall life expectancy at 79.4 years. Women in the US have an average lifespan of 80.2 years, while men average just 74.8 years. This is considerably lower than in comparable nations. Several factors contribute to this disparity, including gun-related violence, homicide, drug-related deaths, suicide, chronic disease, and high-risk occupations. Alongside diet and lifestyle, these elements play a direct role in the lower life expectancy of American men compared to their counterparts in other nations.

Despite enjoying the strongest free speech protections, Americans rank lowest in life expectancy among nations with similarly high levels of free speech protection. This discrepancy is particularly pronounced among US males. While these three areas of comparison do not provide a definitive explanation for every aspect of American life that might relate to the prophecy's reference to citizens being "trained to become like rats," they do bring us a step closer to understanding its implications.

This book offers insights into uniquely American influences that help shape life expectancy but does not claim to provide all the answers. Rather, it serves as a reminder that solutions lie in science, education, and policy development. Greater efforts may be necessary in these and other areas to address the societal patterns that paradoxically position the citizens of one of the world's wealthiest and most powerful nations at a disadvantage in life expectancy rankings.

Additionally, the earlier reference to the rejection of Australia's 2023 Indigenous Voice Referendum highlights a cultural distinction between the United States and other nations, such as Australia, which may hold relevance to the prophecy. Australians overwhelmingly voted to sidestep uncomfortable or inconvenient discussions regarding the nation's marginalized Indigenous population, opting instead to avoid confrontation in favor of maintaining social tranquility. There is also a possibility that the marginalization of Indigenous Australians also impacts census data collection, skewing overall results.

If the data is accurate - though not specifically analyzed here - the lack of open dialogue on such issues may contribute to lower stress levels among the majority population. While engaging in difficult conversations can be beneficial, it can also be a significant source of stress.

The Continual Crisis

In Chapter Five I discussed how adversarial nations have used the US open dialogues and reliance on technological systems to breed a growing dissent among the American people. The tools used are collectively referred to as Fifth-Generational Warfare (5GW). 5GW allows the perpetrator of an attack to sit passively by, while the target attacks itself, with tools of manipulation that have been provided by the perpetrator.

However, a society's resilience and strength are fundamentally tied to the integrity and effectiveness of its systems of governance. When governance is transparent, equitable, and adaptable, it fosters trust, unity, and stability, enabling a society to withstand external pressures and internal challenges. Conversely, weak or compromised governance can undermine social cohesion, amplify divisions, and allow vulnerabilities to fester, making the society more susceptible to decay. When it comes to the US, there are many directions in which a finger can be pointed towards a neglect of its citizenry, which has made the society overall, vulnerable.

In the United States, survival of the average individual requires a form of hypervigilance. Without the comprehensive safety nets provided by social benefits, workers' rights, as needed healthcare, and strong educational support frameworks, a person who is not born into privilege will continuously be at the mercy of whatever happens next.

As hyper-partisanship intensifies, social policies fluctuate dramatically from year to year and vary widely across the 50 states - each largely setting its own distinct policies. This growing instability increases the likelihood of radical shifts and lifestyle uncertainty more than ever before. While this may seem exaggerated, it directly relates to stress, and the American lifestyle can be exceptionally taxing for those without privilege.

For the purposes of this book, "privilege" is defined by a low threshold. It refers to a state of pre-existing comfort before an individual's birth. For instance, this includes an environment where neither parent is absent nor struggling with significant financial hardship, mental or physical health challenges, inequality, or other forms of disadvantage.

If a person is born into an environment in which disadvantage is present, the American lifestyle is a constant battle of hypervigilance. Whether it be the attraction to tabloid journalism, 2-yearly election cycles, constant political bickering, and crisis after crisis from natural disasters, impending wars, gun crime, cultural divisions, conspiracy theories, America is always front-page news across the world. Partly due to its cultural preference for open dialogue. But also, because it is quite entertaining (and/or terrifying) for people in other countries to watch America continually in crisis mode.

There is a well-known Canadian saying that living near the United States is like "living upstairs from a crack house." This phrase is attributed to Canadian author and social activist Pierre Berton. He used this analogy to describe the challenges and influences Canada faces sharing a border with the United States. It does raise the question: if living above the crack house is stressful, what is it like living inside the crack house?

Couple this with "the American Dream", a carrot consisting of economic opportunity, homeownership, education, freedom and equality, which is constantly dangled in front of every American via television and movies, product advertising, and social media influencers. Promoting hard work ethics, competitive drive, protest and resistance, and never giving up. An exhausting combination of factors for any person to endure, every day of their lives. A typical combination of factors for most Americans. Americans, most of whom do not meet the test of having been born into privilege.

Hypervigilance is a state of increased alertness and heightened sensitivity to one's surroundings. It often involves constantly scanning the environment for potential threats or dangers, even when there is no immediate risk. This condition can be a symptom of various mental health disorders, including post-traumatic stress disorder (PTSD), anxiety disorders, and schizophrenia. Hypervigilance is closely linked to chronic stress. And this is where the phrase "become like rats" comes in.

For many years I was perplexed by the prophecy's reference to Americans becoming like rats. The more I examined the way the prophecy was worded and how I remembered the overall messaging, the more I recognised that the term "rats" was not intended to be derogatory. The rest of the prophecy is in no way judgemental, and I was even able to find sufficient precedent to show that the phrase "unholy alliance" was offered without judgement. And so, I went looking for answers in a symbolised place that we often associate with rats: the laboratory.

The American Laboratory

The prophecy declares that the people will be "trained to become like rats," prompting an exploration into the various ways in which rats are conditioned. Rats can be trained for numerous purposes, such as being tamed into suitable domestic pets or learning to perform tricks in exchange for treats. While there may be lesser-known or obscure methods of rat training, the most widely recognised association is their use in laboratory settings.

The word "train" can be aligned with laboratory experiments in multiple ways, particularly in fields like biology, psychology and AI development.

In pharmacology or genetics, certain cells or organisms can be trained to react to certain stimuli. The training occurs when the organism begins to adapt itself relevant that that stimulus over time. Rats are frequently used in biological research due to their genetic similarity to humans, rapid reproduction, adaptability, and suitability for studying various diseases and drug effects.

In psychology or neuroscience, scientists often train animals in controlled experiments to observe learning patterns and responses. Rats are commonly used in behavioural science experiments due to their intelligence, adaptability, and brain structures that share similarities with primitive elements of the human brain, making them valuable models for studying learning, memory, and psychological conditions.

In computer science, researchers train artificial intelligence models by exposing them to large datasets, refining algorithms through repeated experiments. Rats have been used in AI development, particularly in studies related to behavioural learning and vision processing. Researchers have drawn inspiration from operant conditioning, a concept that involves reward and punishment. In operant conditioning, positive reinforcement encourages a behaviour by adding a reward, while negative reinforcement strengthens it by removing an unpleasant stimulus.

The idea that the American population might be experiencing conditions akin to laboratory training is rooted in the way societal forces shape behavior through environmental stimuli, stress, media influence, and political dynamics. Like rats in controlled experiments, individuals are conditioned by hyper-politics, social tensions, and economic pressures, leading to predictable reactions to rewards and punishments, such as economic incentives, news cycles, or algorithm-driven media consumption.

The constant exposure to stressors, ranging from financial instability to health concerns, mirrors operant conditioning, in which responses are shaped by repeated reinforcement. Over time, lifestyle patterns, reduced life expectancy, and psychological strain may resemble the adaptations observed in lab-controlled rats, raising questions about autonomy and systemic influence.

Maslow's Hierarchy of Needs

American psychologist, Abram Maslow, in his 1943 paper called *A Theory of Human Motivation* introduced a five-tier model of human needs that over time has expanded to include as many as 8 distinct tiers. Maslow's hierarchy of needs theory appears in a pyramid design, an example of which is provided below.

The bottom or first level of needs placement is the widest or largest, and the top or final placement is the narrowest or smallest. The theory states that the lower levels of human needs are the supporting framework for any higher levels. If the lower levels are left unfulfilled, the more difficult it is for a person to achieve subsequent, higher levels of needs.

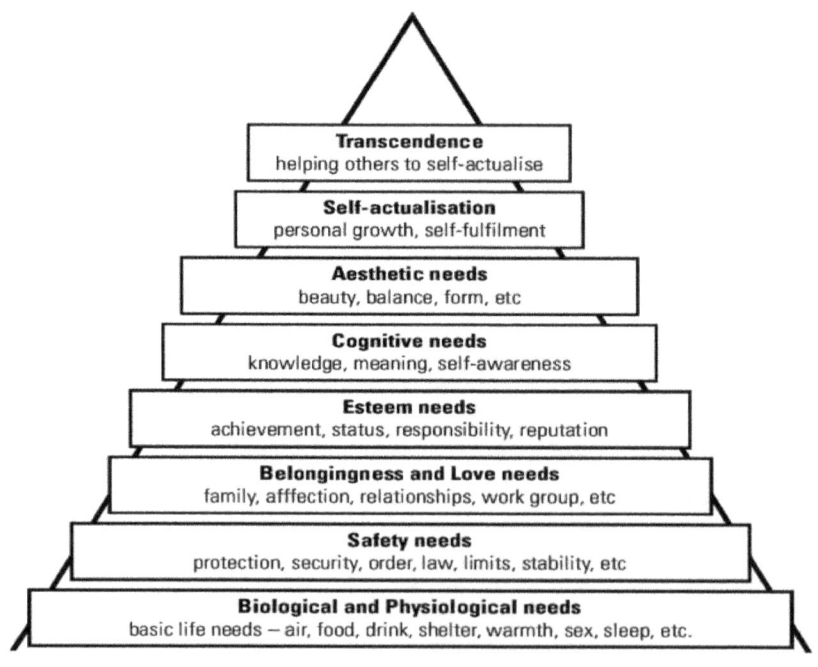

At the foundation of human needs lie biological and physiological necessities, which are the most fundamental for survival. These include essential life components such as air for respiration, shelter for protection, and adequate sleep for well-being. Sex is also considered foundational, for reproductive continuation of the species. When these basic needs are unmet, individuals remain in a state of survival mode, struggling to function beyond immediate survival. This condition can be observed in war-zone populations, individuals experiencing homelessness, and those suffering from untreated illnesses that severely disrupt breathing or sleep.

Safety is the second most fundamental human need. It encompasses both physical and emotional security. A person's sense of safety is shaped by various factors, including the stability of their neighbourhood, access to healthcare, financial preparedness for emergencies, and job security. When these elements are uncertain or compromised, individuals may experience heightened stress and insecurity, impacting their overall wellbeing.

The third fundamental human need centres on love and a sense of belonging. This includes interpersonal relationships, acceptance by others, family connections, and the feeling of being part of a larger collective - whether through spirituality or community involvement. When these social bonds are nurtured, individuals experience greater emotional well-being and a deeper sense of purpose.

Before an individual can fully pursue the higher levels of Maslow's hierarchy, their physiological, safety, and belonging needs must first be met. Biological necessities like air, food, water, sleep, and shelter provide the foundation for survival. Safety and security, including financial stability, health, and protection from harm, ensure a stable environment where a person can function beyond mere survival. Once these are established, social connections such as friendships, family bonds, and community belonging, allow individuals to develop emotional resilience. Without these first three levels, higher aspirations such as self-esteem (level 4), cognitive and aesthetic fulfillment (levels 5 and 6), self-actualization (level 7), and transcendence (level 8) become difficult to achieve, as a person remains preoccupied with addressing their more immediate, foundational needs.

Considering the prophecy's description of people being trained to be like rats, I turned to Maslow's Hierarchy table for understanding. In the United States, the tension between freedom of speech and societal instability may be shaping a form of hypervigilance among its people, especially as crisis management, economic pressures, and declining life expectancy increasingly dominate daily life. While open dialogue fosters self-exploration and innovation, lagging social support systems and ongoing societal stressors create an environment where individuals must constantly assess risks, often reacting defensively rather than constructively.

This heightened awareness, much like operant conditioning, reinforces survival-focused behaviours that, over time, are likely to have undermined collective trust, social cohesion, and long-term stability. As the people have remained locked in a cycle of reaction rather than progress, the foundational resilience of American society has weakened, leading to further divisions, burnout, and systemic vulnerability.

Checking Out

At the same time, Maslow's fourth level in its hierarchy of needs is being exploited by the technology sector. This fourth level relates to a person's self-esteem. Esteem includes an individual's need for self-respect and recognition from others, encompassing feelings of confidence, achievement, and a sense of worth, which contribute to personal growth and societal validation.

This is a complex issue that could warrant an entire book of its own. However, within the US population, there are individuals who have disengaged from the ongoing crises unfolding in news media and other forums. These individuals have essentially "checked out" of a system that fosters hypervigilance.

Yet, disengagement carries its own risks. Those who take the world for granted - going about their days largely unaware of the realities of modern life - risk being blindsided by the creeping influence of technology. Whether disconnected by choice or simply young and inexperienced, they often fail to see how technology is quietly eroding key aspects of their humanity: their self-worth, their sense of personal achievement, and their ability to think critically.

At the same time, they are being behaviourally conditioned. While they may escape the immediate stress of hypervigilance, this detachment comes at a cost: the gradual loss of individual empowerment.

The Replace-Me Generation

The increasing emphasis on technological augmentation, including artificial intelligence, subtly reinforces the idea that an individual's natural abilities are insufficient, fostering a growing sense of inadequacy. As people are encouraged to rely on enhancements to remain competitive, their self-worth becomes increasingly tied to external innovations, eroding confidence in their own innate capabilities and deepening feelings of disposability in an AI-driven world.

As people increasingly turn away from traditional, mainstream learning platforms, they are embracing self-directed learning paths at a growing rate. Many now rely on social media for news updates or experience the world through videos rather than direct engagement. In an era dominated by AI-generated, algorithmically curated content, the information shaping cognitive development is becoming increasingly generic, potentially weakening critical thinking and intellectual growth.

This is a direct threat to Maslow's fifth level of human need: cognitive development. In this environment, the American people resemble subjects in a vast social experiment, conditioned to seek validation and knowledge from unreliable sources, and each other, as a substitute for unmet or actively suppressed fundamental needs. This cycle of reactionary adaptation is unsustainable, leaving the United States increasingly vulnerable to external manipulation and internal fragmentation.

To unravel the puzzle posed by this part of the prophecy, I first sought to better understand rats. What quickly became apparent was that, under chronic stress - especially in overcrowded, resource-scarce environments - rats resort to cannibalism.

Similarly, in the absence of socialist safety nets, amid a perpetual state of crisis, and with an ingrained culture of open dialogue, the ever-present lure of the American Dream, and a complex system of reward and punishment incentives together create a framework for hypervigilance. This is a symptom of chronic stress where individuals perceive themselves in competition with others for basic survival.

And then there are those who remain blindfolded, unaware of the very system they are contained within.

This section of the prophecy speaks to the phenomenon of Americans turning against one another because of escalating hypervigilance and gradual redundancy, until it reaches a tipping point of perceived imminent danger and learned helplessness. This may stem from the erosion of rights and freedoms, the absence of adequate support systems, the accumulation of crises too numerous to withstand, and a growing demand to find synthetic solutions.

Whether the conflict centres on politics, resources, or other societal tensions, it signifies an internal battle raging within the United States. At the time of writing this book, America is experiencing sustained attacks on its Constitutional framework from multiple fronts - many of which originate from within its own borders.

It is also worth noting that 5GW, as discussed in Chapter Five, operates on the principle of allowing a society to consume itself through relentless discord. This dynamic was difficult to overlook and may be contributing to the foundational decay of the West, as described in the prophecy.

Adversarial nations and external agents of chaos are not the only forces eroding the United States from within. Americans are being turned against one another by their own fellow citizens. At the same time, they are being conditioned to believe they are inferior to synthetic alternatives, further weakening them from within. The threat is not solely external. It is domestic.

Chapter Eight
Doomed Nations

> *On the day after Europe's downfall, the United States, at its time of greatest weakness, will be attacked on its own soil by Russia and China [and another] for what will be the first time, but not the last.*

This section of the prophecy describes a moment of time during which the United States is at its weakest, immediately following a day that marks significant disruption to the entire European region.

On the face of it, it is a terrifyingly apocalyptic prediction for anyone living in the West, or allied to the West, and of course for anyone living in the United States or Europe specifically. The words evoke a sense of dread, as though the entire Western Alliance will be overcome by a massive attack, such as would occur during a world war.

However, when this section of the prophecy is examined in greater detail, it becomes less clear. I have spent some time over recent years looking at other prophecies that I could find that predicted some type of European downfall, which appears to be a preliminary feature that must occur. It was surprising to see just how long this prediction has been resurfacing, and in what context.

The European Downfall is Nigh

There has been ongoing prediction about the end of the European establishment order for well over 2000 years. The words used, as translated from their originating source to English are many. They appear in a variety of prophecies dating back to the Early Common Era (ECE).

For the purposes of this book, I have tried to maintain a relative calm when it comes to the topic of a societal downfall. In fact, the word "downfall" is my own, because I am not confident about the exact term what was used in this section of the prophecy.

In the many years that I have searched for the source of this prophecy I have encountered numerous others that share a common prediction of European downfall. The words used to describe such a downfall can be interpreted in wide-ranging ways.

Here are the most common examples:

Collapse is a word that conveys a sudden and systematic breakdown of political and societal structures.

Decay suggests a slow degradation, whether it be moral, social or political. Decay is a word generally attributed to the overall civilisation of Europe, relating to behaviours, health, geography, or institutional factors.

Downfall is the term I have used because, in my view it encompasses many other possible descriptors, but is non-specific. Downfall derives from the classic term *fall* which generally describes a new regime overthrowing an old regime. For example, "the fall of a great empire". Downfall also infers a "pride before the fall" concept, or moral decay and ruin, which helps to place it in the correct context for the prophecy, which seemed to include a similar message.

Other terms I have seen in specific prophetic writings are *dissolution, destruction, ruin, disintegration, annihilation, devastation, fragmentation, cataclysm, and dismantling*. As you can see, there are many and as with anything interpreted from an original ethnic or ancient source, the exact wording may vary, depending on who is doing the interpreting.

What is most notable about each of the many prophecies I have encountered is that those which are most enduring over time, have generally included an aspect of European downfall. The following examples are not the entire range of prophecies to be found; however, they are a collective representation of those relevant to the prophecy discussed in this book that have existed over the past two millennia.

The Sibylline Oracles

Attributed to an enigmatic female oracle by the name of "Sibyl" the Sibylline Oracles are a composite collection of prophetic writings by a variety of different authors and which evolved over centuries. They are a patchwork of texts which draw from pagan, Hellenistic, Judaic and Christian notions of divine judgement. Although their precise origins are complex, they are among the oldest texts associated with apocalyptic prediction.

The oracles are believed to have roots in ancient Greek prophetic traditions, going back to as early as 300 BC. The writings were later absorbed, reworked and expanded upon as they passed into the hands of Roman and early Christian communities. The texts mix poetic imagery of natural disasters, cosmic reordering and moral decay. The writings frequently use words translated to mean "fall", "collapse", or "annihilation". They carry undertones of warning against human institutions considered by many at the time to be overly prideful or corrupt. The prophecies generally stated that such institutions would inevitably face a divine justice, born from vengeance and divine retribution.

Instead of providing a strict chronological forecast, the oracles speak of a cyclical timeline of events. They include hints of recurring patterns in which a regime shall end at the hands of divine punishment, only to be replaced by a renewal of spiritual order. Over time, the new order would become aged, leading to a repeated pattern of replacement and renewal. The oracles offer no firm calendar dates, but retrospectively, they have been aligned with the rise and fall of empires, including empires once existing in Europe. In fact, many passages originally referred to the fall of pagan empires. Later generations, particularly during the medieval period, reworked the prophetic predictions as representing the decline of old orders from the past. In medieval Europe, when social and political crises abounded, a sense of urgency appeared within the prophecies. Vivid predictions about the downfall of great powers gave rise to language such as "signs of the times". This helped to transition and centralise the overall theme of the oracles so that they became a description of instability and eventual collapse of Europe's political and cultural foundations. Moral decay was generally a sign of the final phase of the prophecy coming true, denoting that collapse was drawing near.

Joachim of Fiore's Eschatological Vision

Joachim of Fiore (1135-1200 approx.) was an Italian visionary theologian whose writings profoundly shaped medieval apocalyptic thought. His views on divine progression and the placement of historical events offered a framework that many have since believed to be a foretelling of the collapse of the European establishment order.

Joachim's theories were formed around the proposal that history unfolds in accordance with divinely ordained epochs. His vision was fundamentally linear rather than cyclical. It divided history into three successive epochs, which Joachim believed represented a definitive progression toward an ultimate state of spiritual renewal. In his view, each epoch is given away to the next in a unique unfolding of divine history. Although there may be cyclical metaphors or echoes of recurrence within each epoch, Joachim's model did not see history as an endless loop of repetition but rather as a one-way journey toward a transformative climax.

The Age of the Father

Joachim's theories relate The Age of the Father to the ancient, foundational period depicted in the Old Testament. In this epoch, divine revelation is primarily conveyed through strict laws, patriarchal authority, and the foundations of covenant. Joachim saw this age as one ruled by a paternal order where tradition, ritual, and divine justice set the parameters of human society. It is a time marked by a clear, almost immutable cosmic order, in which human communities are bound by inherited customs and spiritual duty. He believed this early age to be a sturdy framework that provided the necessary structure from which later epochs could emerge and evolve.

The Age of the Son

The Age of the Son relates to our current age. It signifies the historical period inaugurated by the incarnation and ministry of Christ, channelling the ideals and institutions of the Church into the fabric of everyday life. During this epoch, divine truth is embodied in the human realm through the establishment of organized religion, where the sacred and the secular become intertwined. Joachim viewed this period as one of both revelation and decline. He considered that the manifestation of divine love through Christ would be accompanied by the inevitable corruption and institutional decay that arise when human power takes root. Worldly imperfection, blended with spiritual promise, is deemed to set the stage for the transformative shift needed to achieve the next epoch.

The Age of the Holy Spirit

The Age of the Holy Spirit is the anticipated, transformative epoch that promises a profound spiritual awakening and the dissolution of hierarchical rigidities. In this envisioned age, Joachim foresaw Humanity's relationship with the divine transcending traditional structures, giving way to an era of intuitive wisdom, egalitarian spirit, and collective renewal. Joachim's prediction for the Age of the Holy

Spirit was utopian. He believed that each person is destined to experience direct communion with the divine. This would lead to a harmonious, spiritually enlightened society, free from the corruption and dogma that existed in the two previous ages. Joachim likened the 3rd epoch to an era of emancipation involving a convergence of mystical and material matters, and where all of Humanity would reach a time of universal understanding and compassion.

Joachim's writings were likely to be influenced by his personal experiences living in Europe amid the political and social turbulence occurring in medieval times. He was a fervent devotee of Scripture and became known for a variety of other writings and diagrams depicting the ordered process of history, in accordance with biblical writings. His ideas resonated powerfully during a time when many Europeans were living in a period of internal strife, societal upheaval. Interpreters of Joachim's writings saw the works to be a description of Europe tinkering on brink of radical transformation. They envisaged a collapse of everything that ailed them, including the old institutions that they felt imprisoned by, and many lived in preparation for a heavenly intervention and divine reordering of the world.

Joachim's framework did not translate into a modern calendar of events. Instead, he implied that the transition from the Age of the Son to the Age of the Holy Spirit was imminent and unstoppable. A divine progression of history, as certain as the transition from Spring to Summer, or Summer to Fall.

The Prophecies of Nostradamus

Michel de Nostredame, better known as Nostradamus, was a French apothecary and seer who lived through the turbulent years of the Renaissance (1503-1566).

The era in which Nostradamus lived was marked by religious wars, social upheaval and shifting political alliances. He was deeply influenced by provocations of thought, as were many other intellectuals and scholars during this period. This included the widespread fascination with astrology which Nostradamus deeply integrated into celestial themes and visions.

In 1555 Nostradamus published his most pivotal works, *Les Prophéties,* consisting of 942 cryptic verses, commonly referred to as "quatrains". His verses were deliberately vague, intertwining allegorical language with astrological references and historical or mythical symbolisms. Unlike the cyclical Sybilline Oracles, or the linear timelines of Joachim Fiore's epochs, the predictions by Nostradamus lacked any form of discernible structure, which allowed them to remain entirely open to interpretation.

Some quatrains evoke powerful images of calamities, societal decay and the eventual breakdown of established orders. Following Nostradamus's death, interpreters of his works have found what they believe to be links to a European collapse. However, the way Nostradamus weaved together themes of natural disaster, internal corruption and external conflicts such as war, suggests that it could apply to any major civilization that exists within a cycle of crises or transformation.

Nostradamus did not provide explicit dates or chronology within his writings. His predictions were cryptic and heavily coded. Subsequent mapping has aligned various verses to known historical events relating to significant milestones in European history. One often-cited prediction from Nostradamus describes the rise of a tyrannical figure who would unleash great suffering across Europe. The prediction was interpreted by some to be a reference to Adolf Hitler and the chaos of World War One. The vivid imagery of upheaval and destruction in his quatrains has been retrospectively seen as a foretelling of the brutality inside European during that time in history.

Perhaps it is the allure of the mysterious, which helps to keep the predictions of Nostradamus alive and well even today. Nonetheless, the open-ended nature of his prophecies allows for universal applicability, which seems to have appeal to many people for many generations. He is, perhaps, the best-known prophet of all time, even if the fluid, interpretative framework of his predictions allows them to be superimposed on a wide range of scenarios. His legacy ensures precisely because his words resonate with an enduring human preoccupation with the rise and fall of power, much of which has been a controlling and limiting aspect of human life.

The Fatima Prophecies

In 1917, amid the global conflict of World War One, three shepherd children, Lucia dos Santos and her cousins Jacinta and Francisco

Marto, began reporting extraordinary visions. They lived in the small town of Fatima in central Portugal. The visions involved Marian apparitions in which a beautiful ethereal woman in white would appear, like a floating hologram in the sky.

The Marian apparitions were officially recognised by the Catholic Church as divine miracles and a call to repentance and religious conversion. The events at Fatima resonated with many as a direct message from the divine, echoing centuries of prophetic writings, whilst also speaking directly of a modern crisis. The reported phenomena appeared at a time when societies were grappling with rapid political, societal and religious change. This made the events in Fatima a symbol of both urgent warnings, and enduring hope.

Contained within the phenomena were messages conveyed by what was interpreted to be a visitation by the Virgin Mary, known as the "three secrets". The first secret offered a stark vision of Hell and described the eternal consequences of sin and moral decay afflicting humanity. The second secret was a forecast of a major conflict, which has since been interpreted to be a prediction of World War Two. It included a dire warning that an even more devastating catastrophe was to come if humanity didn't learn from the ravages of the second world war, and if people continued to stray from their divine purpose.

The third secret was withheld from the public for many decades and was purported to be known only by an adult Lucia dos Santos and a handful of Vatican insiders. It was later revealed to be a calling for Christian believers to remain steadfast in their faith as Europe entered a period of transformative crisis and eventual renewal.

Unlike the cyclical frameworks of earlier prophecies, the Fatima prophecies were deeply anchored in modern history. The second secret is commonly believed to relate to World War Two, a conflict that reshaped Europe and the global order of the 20th century. Some interpretations of the first and third secrets also claim a connection to the Cold War during which the advancement of communism occurred in Eastern Europe.

The Fatima prophecies act as a kind of bridge between medieval prophecy and modern apocalyptic discourse. It has also helped to embed a theme of "good versus evil" into discussions of politics, society and international relations. It is an example of a phenomenon that exerts a profound influence on modern Christian, particularly Catholic, spirituality. Enduring legacies included ongoing debates and perceptions about the existence of divine intervention in the past, present or future, and the moral direction of modern Europe.

The blend of urgent warning with a promise of spiritual renewal continues to inspire people of faithful religious devotion and non-religious spiritual reflection. It helps to uphold the idea that any period of crisis or hardship is an opportunity for profound spiritual transformation.

For me personally, and despite my non-religious and somewhat sceptical perspective, it is difficult to reconcile the Fatima event. I am suspicious of the third secret's eventual revelations which I believe could have easily been contrived and manipulative. However, I cannot discount the phenomena as reported. The three children who witnessed the earlier apparitions took their testimonies to the grave.

And, the final event, in which a "miracle of the sun" occurred, was reportedly witnessed by tens of thousands of people, and occurred at precisely the time and place that had been predicted by "Our Lady of Fatima" during the previous sighting.

Baba Vanga

Baba Vanga (1911-1996) stands as one of Eastern Europe's most famous seers. Her predictions have attracted considerable popular attention over the decades. Her prophecies differ significantly from those of Nostradamus and the Fatima apparitions, in several ways.

Firstly, Baba Vanga's visions were rooted in the folk traditions and mystical culture of the Balkans rather than in a formal theological or literary way.

Secondly, unlike her counterparts Nostradamus and those behind the Fatima prophecies, Baba Vanga's predictions possessed a distinctly populist, mythical quality. While they may have been recorded in various formats over time, they were initially known because Vanga foretold them contemporaneously, delivering them in the moment.

In stark contrast, Nostradamus meticulously crafted his cryptic quatrains, each designed to invite layers of interpretation. Meanwhile, the Fatima secrets diverge from Vanga's visions by being deeply embedded in modern Catholic thought, shaping religious perspectives in ways her prophecies did not.

Baba Vanga's predictions ranged in topic, from natural disasters to geopolitical upheavals, and often included symbolic language which made them open to multiple interpretations. For many people in Eastern Europe, her words resonate with a kind of foundational intuition about the destiny of the region. Populist pride, mixed with heavy symbolism and mystery gives Vanga's prophecies a distinctly romantic quality that compensates for any lack of institutional validation or written official recording.

In terms of influencing Europe's future in prophetic narratives, Baba Vanga's predictions have struck a chord by echoing similar themes of crisis, fragmentation, and renewal that appear in other prophetic traditions. According to some interpretations, she foresaw the radical transformation of established institutions across Europe, or the destruction of those structures entirely. These interpretations of Vanga's visions align to the apocalyptic thought that dominated medieval prophecies.

The Outlier

Having compared many of the enduring prophets, such as Nostradamus, Baba Vanga and others, it becomes clear how they all find commonality in the overall foretelling of global power shift and European demise.

However, there are also distinct differences between them, and a single outstanding feature of the 1980s prophecy which is the focus of this book.

The differences are easiest explained when viewed from three specific vantage points, as follows.

Cultural v. Doctrinal Authority

In many ways, Baba Vanga's predictions have permeated popular culture, providing a rich source of discussion on news networks, internet forums, and books that explore apocalyptic themes. This contrasts with the more doctrinal or scholarly approaches taken when interpreting Nostradamus or the Fatima secrets. Her impact on societal perspectives is often more about inspiring conversation and invoking a sense of mystery around Europe's destiny rather than offering a clearly articulated, church-endorsed roadmap.

This is not to say that Nostradamus or the Fatima secrets are more valid than the Vanga's visions. However, they have achieved a structured framework of examination by historians or theologians that has not yet been achieved by Vanga.

In comparison, Vanga's influence of often more pronounced in popular culture and among segments of society that cherish mystical or alternative insights rather than perspectives that align to organised religion or academia. Scholars tend to treat her prophecies as part of a broader tapestry of folklore, rather than definitively predictive. The Fatima and Nostradamus predictions have been strongly debated in academic circles. This has elevated the overall perception of credibility, among those who possess an assumption of authority on the matter of prophecy analysis.

Institutional Endorsement

There is some overlap here with the previous point, however it also should be noted that the Fatima apparitions have been extensively studied, debated and even endorsed as confirmed "miracles" by official channels and means of the Catholic Church. This fact contributes to a sense of solemn urgency and divine intervention in a historical sense. Baba Vanga's legacy is more that of a cherished folk mystic. Her words inspire and call for vigilance, but they are less likely to be integrated into official or scholarly narratives about Europe's future. Nostradamus sits somewhere between the two other prophets. His curious quatrains are considered by theologians and historians alike, to be worthy of close examination, but not to the point of official validation or endorsement.

Methodology and Precision

Of the three enduring prophets, Nostradamus has the most carefully structured predictions, involving layers messaging using multiple verses and symbols. Similarly, the Fatima secrets are layered with symbolism that invite systematic analysis. This structuring has allowed both Nostradamus and Fatima to be closely examined and potentially linked to historical events, albeit retrospectively.

Baba Vanga's predictions are far less formalised. This means that while they certainly add to the discourse of European prophetic traditions, they tend to be more malleable and can be reshaped to fit contemporary events or anxieties.

The prophecy which is the focus of this book has a single element that makes it stand out from all others I have seen during the years that I have been searching for answers. It includes specifications that no other prophecy so far seems to include. The two men with 5 letters in their last names, the timeline of European downfall and the specific aggressor nations, two-pronged approach and relationship to other countries, are all features that seem unique to this single prophecy. It is the reason why I have found the prophecy to be as compelling as I do, and why it has remained unforgettable over the multi-decade timeline during which I have been aware of it.

Modern Manipulations

There is significant evidence that many prophetic texts, including those from the well-known, enduring examples of Nostradamus, Fatima and Baba Vanga, have been repurposed and manipulated to influence public sentiment. Prophetic texts are famously ambiguous, which allows for virtually any contemporary event to be retrofitted to support a particular narrative. In today's digital age, the ambiguity of prophecy has propelled many a personal career or political agenda, making the manipulation of prophecy a fertile breeding ground for opportunism. The 3 Europe-based prophets discussed in this chapter provide particularly well-worn examples of message manipulation.

Following are 3 examples of how the cited prophecies have been recently manipulated in online forums.

Nostradamus predicts the "End of the European Order"

Following significant geopolitical events, including the Cold War's culmination resulting in the dissolution of the Soviet Union (1991), the 9/11 terrorist attacks in New York (2001), and the Brexit vote (2016), a revisiting of the Nostradamus quatrains took place. Online forums and social media often highlighted references to "great kings" and "terror" as signs pointing to Europe's imminent collapse.

Propagandists and political commentators repurposed ambiguous lines from Nostradamus texts and retrofitted them to the events of the time, presenting them as evidence to support the narrative of inevitable collapse. These retro-interpretations fuelled alarmist narratives that led to the growing distrust of European institutions, and a bolstering of populist arguments. Everything happens in a nanosecond online, so the result was the rapid spread of polarised debate about Europe's future. The future of the United States was often a major player in the narrative, linking Europe's impending demise to US events.

Fatima predicts "Cultural Renewal"

Stemming from the Marian apparitions at Fatima in 1917, the Fatima secrets have long been intertwined with calls for repentance and renewal within the Catholic community. In the modern era, themes drawn from these visions have been mobilised amid debates over immigration, secularisation and cultural identity.

All over the world, right-wing and traditionalist groups have long emphasized warnings from Fatima. The events of 1917, having been recognised by the Church as being worthy of belief, they were often linked to the prospects of divine retribution against perceived moral decay. Social media campaigns, online documentaries and activist literature have selectively framed Fatima's messages as indications of a coming crisis if secular influence is left unchecked. This has reinforced conservative political narratives, and galvanized segments of the Christian population. Many continue to believe, even today, that fighting secularized thinking is a divine mission, and part of the higher quest to save Humanity from itself. It subsequently becomes impossible to oppose or debate, or at times question, the Christian cause, when some segments of Christianity see themselves as heroic characters in a divine battle against evil.

Bava Vanga's annual prediction of "Impending Doom"

A favourite among tabloid journalists, conspiracy theorists and online influencers, Baba Vanga's predictions are often, perhaps routinely, manipulated with the use of memes, videos and speculative articles. These methods are used to reinterpret her vague prophecies as precise predictions for events such as the collapse of the European Union, economic meltdowns, or even global pandemics.

I have personally been monitoring the annual predictions made by Baba Vanga since she died in 1996. Each year, she appears, resurrected to predict the calamities of the world in the coming year. The format is almost always the same as the previous year. The messaging will generally appear in January, as the new year begins. There will be a declaration of accuracy from the past, wherein a major event such as the COVID-19 pandemic was retrofitted into her predictions, followed by predictions about natural disasters, institutional collapse and a shift in the global order. These reinterpretations almost ways permeate a variety of online communities, particular among groups who may have a predisposition to distrust official narratives. The viral spread of these repurposed messages has contributed to a climate of fear and scepticism about the future of Europe, often intersecting with broader conspiratorial discourse surrounding China, Russia and the United States.

Echo Chambers and Viral Narratives

Social media platforms, blogs and online forums create spaces where ambiguous prophecies are continuously discussed, reinterpreted and embellished. In many cases, this leads to echo chambers in which a particular interpretation, most often the apocalyptic or conspiratorial variety, spreads unchecked. Memes, hashtags and viral videos have all played a role in aligning ancient warnings with current fears about global instability or the decline of traditional values.

The prevalence and success of these echo chambers should not go unnoticed and can be easily seen firsthand by searching terms such as "prophecy" or "predictions" in places like TikTok, YouTube, or Facebook, and comparing subscriber, view and comment counts. The videos and blogs that contain inflammatory language and imagery in thumbnails or headlines, will invariably have more subscribers, views and comments, than simple or generic content that seeks to inform and educate, rather than invoke fear. Equal only to sex, fear and anxiety sells. It is for this reason that I chose to provide as much information and context as possible in this book. Whether I do it well or poorly, my intention has always been to highlight the uncanny aspects of the prophecy that I encountered 4 decades ago, whilst also attempting to maintain a sense of precision, purpose and accountability.

Political and Cultural Agendas

In various instances, political movements and cultural commentators have intentionally drawn on prophecy to underscore their critiques or to mobilise support. For example, reinterpretations of Nostradamus and Fatima have been cited in discussions about national identity, immigration and perceived cultural decay in both the United States and Europe (and probably other countries as well). By selectively referencing these sources, public figures can lend an air of divine inevitability to their warnings, thereby intensifying public concern, and polarising opinion.

Media and Misinformation

With the rise of the internet, traditional gatekeepers like academic journals and institutional analyses have often been bypassed in favour of rapid, sensationalised content. This environment has enabled misinformation to be inadvertently, and purposefully, manipulated and then widely circulated. As misinformation reaches a broader audience it can significantly influence public discourse, often merging with other conspiracy theories and alarmist narratives. At the time of writing, I am aware of a recent example in which a media forum which self-describes as "fact-based and unbiased" news outlet is airing a report which combines the JFK assassination conspiracy with the UAP disclosure conspiracy. Whether it is a conflation or entirely factual, the prima facie message remains the same: that murder may have been committed to conceal information highly relevant to the public interest and international security.

Overall, and while the original prophetic texts that exist and endure in popular culture carry layers of historical, cultural and symbolic meaning, the modern digital landscape has enabled a kind of rebranding of those prophecies. What was once a matter of nuanced theological debate or mysterious literary expression, has become a potent online tool for instilling fear, raising suspicions about societal structures, and influencing political outcomes.

Modern European downfall

Prophecies predicting Europe's downfall are often grandiose and catastrophic, depicting widespread destruction and devastation—a fate that may indeed unfold as foretold. However, collapse does not always manifest through dramatic upheaval; history reveals that decline can take subtler forms, eroding foundations through political instability, economic fragility, and social fragmentation. Recent events provide compelling examples that illustrate how Europe's transformation might align with these more gradual yet consequential shifts.

Brexit

The Brexit vote, held on June 23, 2016, resulted in 52% of British voters choosing to leave the European Union, marking the first instance of a nation withdrawing from the bloc and sparking years of political negotiations and economic uncertainty. Brexit can be interpreted as a strategic fracture in Europe's unity, aligning with historical prophecies that have long warned of the continent's decline due to political instability, economic turmoil, and internal divisions.

Britain's departure weakened the cohesion of the EU, fuelling nationalist movements and geopolitical shifts that some may see as fulfilling ancient predictions. Rather than an isolated event, Brexit could represent a modern manifestation of Europe's unravelling, as foretold in various prophetic traditions. Moreover, Britain's exit may have been a necessary step in Europe's transformation, potentially laying the groundwork for a more centralized power structure, in line with prophecies warning of conflict and sweeping change. Whether seen as an assault on Europe or an inevitable historical evolution, Brexit undeniably altered the continent's trajectory, reinforcing themes of division, uncertainty, and the struggle for sovereignty that have echoed through centuries of prophecy.

The Pope

The Prophecy of the Popes is a centuries-old document attributed to St. Malachy, a 12th-century Irish archbishop who allegedly had a vision of all future popes. It consists of 112 cryptic Latin phrases, each believed to describe a pope from Malachy's time until the end of the world. The final pope in the prophecy, known as "Peter the Roman," is foretold to lead the Church through great tribulations, culminating in the destruction of Rome and the arrival of divine judgment.

The death of Pope Francis on April 21, 2025, has reignited discussions about prophetic warnings regarding Europe's decline, particularly in relation to the St. Malachy prophecy and broader historical predictions. Some interpretations suggest that Francis was the final pope, marking the onset of a period of turmoil and upheaval for the Catholic Church and, by extension, Europe itself. According to the prophecy, Peter the Roman will guide the Church through immense challenges before the fall of the city of seven hills, a reference many traditionally associate with Rome.

However, the idea of Rome as the city of seven hills may be based on outdated theological alignments, raising the possibility of a different geopolitical interpretation. Other figures, such as Nostradamus, have also been credited with predicting political instability and religious transformation in Europe. His cryptic writings have been linked to the weakening of papal authority, suggesting that the transition to Pope Leo XIV on May 8, 2025, signalled a shift in the Vatican's influence and a broader European decline.

An alternative interpretation suggests that the city of seven hills may not refer to Rome at all but rather to another global power, more relevant to the current era. Some theologians argue that the seven hills align with the seven heads of the beast in biblical prophecy, possibly pointing to the United States as the emerging geopolitical force. This concept is examined more closely in Chapter Ten. However, the selection of an American pope, the first in history, has fuelled speculation that the traditional European dominance of Catholicism is waning, potentially reinforcing prophecies of Europe's diminishing influence on the global stage.

While these prophecies remain open to interpretation, the political, economic, and religious shifts occurring in Europe today undeniably reflect themes of uncertainty, fragmentation, and transformation that have long been foretold. Whether seen through a prophetic lens or as a natural geopolitical evolution, the continent is navigating a critical turning point in its history.

The attack

The prophecy is explicit about both the timing of an attack on the United States and the identities of those responsible. However, beyond striving for an accurate interpretation of its message, I have not undertaken an extensive investigation into what may unfold next. In my view, attempting to predict future events in isolation of universal laws is a misguided endeavour. It assumes that the future is predetermined, fixed in time and space, and incapable of change.

These are notions I do not subscribe to, which may seem paradoxical coming from a tarot enthusiast. However, I believe something far more complex is at play - a perspective I explore later in this book and one that I am certain will provide deeper insight into why I hold this belief.

My focus has always been on understanding the deeper purpose and intention of this and other prophecies. Not merely the events they foretell, but the patterns and clues embedded in past occurrences. These historical insights serve as guiding markers, helping us anticipate challenges and navigate the uncertainties of what lies ahead.

The day after

In biblical prophecy, a "day" is often interpreted as representing one year, based on passages such as Ezekiel 4:6 wherein it states, "*I have assigned you a day for each year*", and Numbers 14:34 that says, "*For forty years - one year for each of the forty days"*. This day-year principle is commonly applied in prophetic timelines, particularly in books like Daniel and Revelation, where symbolic periods such as 70 weeks or 1,260 days are understood by some scholars to signify years rather than literal days.

The United States is described in the prophecy as being at "its time of greatest weakness", when it is "attacked on its own soil by Russia, China [and another]." Interestingly, there is a recent precedent for this having possibly occurred.

Europe in 2019

In 2019, Europe experienced a series of political, economic, and social upheavals the most prominent of which was Brexit. Despite Brexit's initiation having dated back to 2016, a sudden and deepening uncertainty in the European Union occurred after Prime Minister Theresa May's Withdrawal Agreement was rejected on January 15, 2019.

Compounding with the rejection of May's Agreement, ongoing protests in France, fuelled by economic inequality and public dissatisfaction, continued into 2019, exposing deeper fractures within the European social fabric. At the same time, economic stagnation and concerns over financial instability left Europe vulnerable to global shocks, setting the stage for broader shifts in geopolitical power.

Europe saw a sudden rise in authoritarianism in 2019, particularly with the growing influence of far right and nationalist movements across multiple countries. Reports highlighted how authoritarian parties gained ground in national elections, with some securing positions in the European Parliament elections on May 26, 2019. These parties, including those in France, Hungary, Germany, Italy, and Poland, were criticized for their anti-democratic policies, financial scandals, and links to oligarchs. Additionally, Hungary's Prime Minister Viktor Orbán continued to push his vision of "illiberal democracy," which involved restrictions on free speech, press freedoms, and human rights organizations. This trend reflected a broader shift toward nationalist and authoritarian governance, challenging traditional democratic norms in Europe.

At the same time, tension between Ukraine and Russia began to escalate. While Russia had already been involved in the Donbas conflict since 2014, 2019 saw continued hostilities. Throughout the year, Russian-backed separatists engaged in clashes with Ukrainian forces, leading to over 110 Ukrainian soldiers killed. On February 20, 2019, Ukraine officially classified 7% of its territory as "temporarily occupied" due to Russian influence. It would still be a few years until Russia launched a full-scale invasion of Ukraine, marking the most significant military conflict in Europe since WORLD WAR TWO. However, the tone had been set by these multiple factors affecting Europe's geopolitical shifts in 2019.

The United States in 2020

One year later, in early 2020, the United States became the epicentre of the COVID-19 pandemic, struggling with unprecedented health, economic, and societal crises that weakened its global standing. As the virus spread, conspiracies emerged about its origins, with some suggesting a lab leak from the Wuhan Institute of Virology in China had led to the pandemic. This was an accusation that intensified tensions between the US and China. Meanwhile, Russia took advantage of the global instability, escalating cyberattacks, disinformation campaigns, and strategic interventions designed to sow division within the United States. These actions, whether seen as direct attacks or opportunistic manoeuvres, contributed to an environment where American power was being challenged in ways that echoed Europe's struggles from the previous year.

Viewed together, the events of 2019 in Europe and 2020 in the US suggest a coordinated global shift, where traditional Western powers faced crises that weakened their influence, allowing new actors, China, Russia, and emerging political movements, to reshape the geopolitical landscape. Whether interpreted through a prophetic lens or geopolitical analysis, this sequence of events highlights a critical moment in global history, where the foundations of power were tested in rapid succession.

It should be noted that the prophecy did refer to a 3rd entity uniting with Russia and China in this section. However, as much as I have tried to recall who the entity is, I have not been able to do so with confidence. It may be another nation, but it may equally be something else. The rise of authoritarianism is provided here as a possible example of a 3rd party not specifically applying to any single nation.

Did the Nazis leave us a clue?

In Chapter Three the "unholy alliance" referred to as the Molotov-Ribbentrop Pact of 1939 illustrated how a marriage of convenience between Adolf Hitler's fascist Germany and Josephe Stalin's communist Soviet Union served its purpose, even though the two powers had previously been bitter enemies. For a period, the Pact provided for Europe to be partitioned off and thereby weakened in such a way as to become vulnerable to widespread attack by both Germany and the Soviet Union, thus facilitating the devastating consequences of World War Two.

In its first 2 years, the Pact seemed to benefit the USSR tremendously. It allowed the Soviets to regain lost territories and expand their influence in Eastern Europe while buying time to build up their military. However, the Pact took a savage and unexpected turn thereafter.

In 1941, Hitler betrayed Stalin by launching Operation Barbarossa, the largest invasion in history at that point. The surprise attack shattered the illusion of cooperation, catching the Soviet forces unprepared and leading to devastating losses.

The betrayal forced the Soviet Union into an existential fight for survival in World War Two, one that ultimately turned the tide against Nazi Germany. But in the short term, it cost the USSR heavily in lives, resources, and national security. The Soviets fought back hard but had been severely handicapped by the surprise factor. They were forced to respond in brutal and relentless ways, which included shifting to full wartime economy. This sacrificed the day-to-day wellbeing of the people in favour of rapid production of weapons and the mobilisation of millions of troops. The Soviets also adopted scorched earth strategies, destroying infrastructure, crops and supplies wherever they went so that advancing German troops would have nothing to survive on. This had a devastating impact on any territory former occupied by Soviet troops.

Ultimately, the Soviets fought their way back and managed to push Nazi retreat into Berlin by 1945. The cost, however, was staggering. Tens of millions of lives were lost.

If Stalin had suspected Hitler's true intentions earlier, things might have unfolded differently. This might be a clue for unholy alliances to follow. The opportunistic ally is an ally that might turn at any moment. Is this a clue related to the prophecy's description of a weakened United States being vulnerable to attack by its unholy ally? Are Russia, China, or the unknown 3rd entity the ally that turns against the United States? Or is it possible that the US is the ally that turns against its own allies, which somehow leads to a pre-emptive strike on the US by an enemy formerly considered a friend?

Finally, this section of the prophecy also states that the attack foretold would take place on US soil is only the first, and that others would follow. This is far less of a surprise than it may seem in the first instance. One premise I have been developing as I continue to investigate the prophecy, is that it appears to be repeating itself in current events. For this reason, any number of foretold events might have occurred before, may be occurring now, and may repeat or occur again in the future.

Chapter Nine
Breaking Old Bonds

> *The West will align to Russia, the East and Oceania to China. The United States will be alone.*

At the time of writing this book it seems unlikely for "the West to align with Russia", or for the multi-lateral relationships between the East and West to homogenise beneath a China-centric umbrella.

The West's relationship with Russia has long since been a complex mixture of cooperation and rivalry, dating back to the era of the Russian Empire. China's relationship with the West is equally complex, shaped by cooperation, competition, and ideological differences.

Economically, China is deeply integrated with Western markets, serving as a global manufacturing hub and trading partner. Politically, tensions arise over issues like human rights, technology, and territorial disputes, leading to moments of friction. Despite disagreements, both sides recognize the necessity of diplomatic engagement, balancing economic interdependence with strategic rivalry. The dynamic continues to evolve as China asserts itself as a global power.

Russia's relationships are "complicated"

Since the fall of the Russian Empire, Russia has maintained significant trade, cultural and political ties with many Western European nations. Russia has also asserted its own distinct identities and interests and has at times asserted itself in ways that the West has opposed. One example is the annexation of Crimea in 2014, when Russia defied European traditions of resolving disputes through peaceful diplomacy. It deployed military forces and orchestrated a highly disputed referendum to seize Ukrainian territory. This was an action that led to widespread international condemnation and the imposition of significant sanctions.

Russia's dual approach, in which it embraces aspects of Western civilisation, while also remaining distinctly at odds with the West overall, means that moments of peaceful partnerships have frequently given way to periods of tension and adversarial conduct.

Ukraine: A shock to the West

Since Russia's invasion of Ukraine in 2022, the conflict has profoundly redefined global alliances. The United States, along with member of the European Union and NATO, have rallied around Ukraine. With few exceptions, the West views Russia's aggression as more than just a regional crisis, but as an attack on the rules-based international order. Since Donald Trump's return to office US-Ukraine relations have sometimes been strained, but at the time of writing, the United States continues to support Ukraine.

The war in Ukraine has sparked an urgent reassessment of security strategies, and a renewed commitment to collective defence. The timing of the conflict (relevant to the COVID-19 pandemic), and the conflict itself has given an unprecedented economic shock to the European energy markets. The effects have reverberated globally, which in turn has solidified the West's response in supporting Ukraine and expanding its own alliances.

NATO: The linchpin of the West

Amid growing concerns over Russian expansionism, NATO members have significantly increased their defence spending. They have bolstered their military presence, especially along Eastern European borders. NATO's enhanced stationing of forces in countries like Poland and the Baltic states reflects a determined effort to send a message to Russia: cross any of these borders and you will ignite a direct conflict with the Alliance.

NATO's coordinated military aid and its careful balancing act of supporting Ukraine while avoiding escalation, reflects its pivotal role in maintaining regional stability and discouraging further aggression.

Diplomacy, sanctions and strategic realignment

The West's key methods of deterring and limiting Russia's ability to easily expand its military operations combines strategies of diplomacy, partnerships and sanction response.

Regular high-level consultations, intelligence sharing and coordinated response are directed towards minimising the impact of cyberattacks and disinformation campaigns against any Western partner. Traditionally, the level of trust between an allied West has been strong. Such a unified approach is essential, not only for stabilising Eastern Europe, but also to project a coherent diplomatic front. It is a key part of the collective defence mechanism and has a significant influence over global security and economic policy.

The economic sanctions utilised by the West against Russia, involve widespread financial restrictions and trade embargoes that are aimed at depriving the Russian government of the very resources it needs to fuel a military operation. The problem with these types of sanctions is that they have twofold effect. Whilst they substantially weaken the Russian economy, they also generate a ripple effect that impacts the global supply chain. This influences international markets and serve to recalibrate global economic alliances. The West, whether it be European partners, the United States, or the wider Western alliance, may all feel the impact of sanctions on their own nation's trading relationships.

The global sands are shifting

Regardless of the efforts to utilise combined carrot and stick methodologies such as diplomacy and sanctions to maintain global stability, a small group of outlier nations will always have a subtle but continuous influence over the continuity of international partnership arrangements. That is the nature of a country's sovereignty. There is only so much an outside country, or group of countries can to do control the inside forces of a sovereign nation. Russia, along with China, and other red-headed stepchildren of the global order, will always find a way to use their state of sovereignty to shift the goalposts.

The emerging influence of BRICS

Over the past several years, BRICS, an acronym for the original five-member collaboration between Brazil, Russia, India, China and South Africa, has evolved significantly in scope and ambition. In 2023, BRICS began extending invitations to more nations. It currently consists of 10 members, having added Indonesia, Iran, Ethiopia, Egypt and the United Arab Emirates to its membership base.

BRICS began in 2009 as an alternative to the G7 economic partnership. It was at first largely symbolic in its inclusiveness of countries with small or emerging economies. Whilst its global trading influence is still second to that of the G7 bloc, its combined GDP is rapidly rising at a rate that many economic forecasters believe will overshadow the combined GDP of G7 nations within a few years. BRICS member nations already represent more than 45% of the world's population, compared to G7, which represents around 10% of the world's population.

The subtle shift in BRICS is that its expansion is driven by ambition to create a partnership that challenges traditional Western financial and political orders and taps into the diverse economic and regional influence of its new members.

The US dollar in the crosshairs

One of the primary economic motives behind the BRICS expansion is the reduction in reliance on the US dollar, a tool that has long underpinned Western dominance in global trade. BRICS member negotiations include initiatives such as the "BRICS Pay System", which decentralises the facilitation of international transactions and allows local currency transactions between nations that would traditionally have to incorporate the US dollar. This initiative serves to diminish the influence of Western financial institutions, particularly those of the United States.

A trend towards multi-polarisation

Beyond economics, the emergence of BRICS as a strategic alternative has served as a representation of a wider shift in geopolitical transformations.

For example, the West has rallied around issues like the Ukraine war, while the BRICS members have rallied around the concept of alternative global governance. This evolving landscape is developing an emerging multipolarity, where global influence is distributed across more countries, and alliances are becoming more fluid. In one key example, Saudia Arabia and the United Arab Emirates, considered to be dominant Mid-Eastern players, have longstanding economic ties to the US. Both are now straddling the fence, balancing their US trade alliances with their growing interest in economic and political relations with BRICS members.

Loyalties are shifting across the world, and nations are feeling less tethered to a single set of economic partnerships. It is the beginning of what appears to be a new multipolar world order. In a multipolar world, no single nation can assume power dominance. Where does that then take the US dollar, and indeed the United States itself, when the global dominance of the US has traditionally been its primary identifier?

Trade wars trending

In recent years, a surge in trade wars and increasing protectionist policies have triggered a recalibration of global economic alliances. Nations are increasingly linking their trade policies to other factors, such as cultural ideology or national security interests.

The United States and Europe have begun favouring trade arrangements with nations in close geographic proximity to themselves. This practice is referred to as "friendshoring" or "nearshoring". It shortens the supply chain, to protect against long-range global trade disputes or military conflicts. While these measures are intended to insulate domestic economies, they are disruptive to established trade flows and force nations outside of the "friendzone" to find alternative markets.

To illustrate the pressure being applied on once firm allied trading partners, the Australian Prime Minister, Anthony Albanese recently made a public statement that the 10% trade tariff imposed by the Trump Administration in retaliation for not accepting US beef imports into Australia, was "not the act of a friend". Prime Minister Albanese, less than one month away from general election, was surprised by the

US President, who began insisting that Australia reverse its policy not to accept US beef due to the biodiversity impact it presents to Australian farmers. The acceptance of a foreign meat raises the risk of an inadvertent spread of "mad cow disease", which has the potential to wipe out Australian farming. The protection against this risk has been a longstanding policy of the Australian government, regardless of political leadership.

Within days of the Prime Minister's public statement, China inserted itself into the discussion by offering Australia an opportunity to expand on its existing trade arrangements, as a means of bypassing the US trade arrangement altogether. Mr Albanese replied that on this occasion Australia would remain in the established US trade relationship. Under Albanese, Australia has been gradually implementing a variety of measures to secure a portion of its critical exports, and to secure a diverse range of trading partners across the world. It did not have to panic buy the offer of a US competitor nation.

However, it could have gone either way. The moment was a brief one, only weeks away from an election, and in this instance the political needle threaded by the Australian leader was fine enough to gather him support of the Australian population just prior to an election, whilst retaining economic relationships with China and the US.

It may not end in the same result next time, or with the next world leader who is placed in this type of situation. Next time, and perhaps in future next times, the result may be to break away from the established economic alliance.

The pivot towards Asia and away from the US

Facing a barrage of sanctions and restrictive trade measures from the West, Russia has pivoted towards Asia to secure its economic interests. This realignment is driven by a need to sustain export revenues relating to energy and raw materials, and to strengthen geopolitical and economic bonds outside the Western region.

Russia is increasing its trade relations with China and India, and these arrangements are bypassing the US dollar, which reduces dependency on Western financial institutions. Other countries that have been isolated from traditional Western markets, whether in Asia, Latin America or Africa, are similarly signing bilateral free-trade agreements that create corridors to bypass the US-centric trade system. The result is a nuanced reordering of the global world order. The more protectionist the West becomes in its sanction-driven isolations, the more non-West nations are finding alternative routes of trade. The favoured direction of travel is to a nation or partnership that is inclusive, increasingly powerful, and where the collective GDP and world population figures are rising exponentially. Extending throughout these frameworks is a nation that meets all criteria: China.

The World Aligns with Russia and China?

While today's global order firmly places Russia at odds with the Western alliance, especially considering the Ukraine conflict, a distant yet thought-provoking scenario aligns to the earliest part of the prophecy. An "unholy alliance" is an alliance that nonetheless forms, despite it ordinarily being seen as improbable, unorthodox or unsavoury. Such an alliance could occur during unexpected circumstances that breed a common interest.

Setting the stage for an unlikely alliance

Historical precedents remind us that international alliances are fluid and often reshaped by extraordinary triggers. To illustrate, Japan and the United States share a strong alliance based on economic cooperation, security collaboration, and diplomatic coordination, with both nations working closely to maintain stability in the Indo-Pacific region. Such an alliance was unforeseeable and likely to be labelled "unholy" immediately following the US bombing of Hiroshima, in 1945. The key difference between today and 80 years ago is that everything changes at a faster pace than it did back then. Competitive drive is fiercer than before, technology is faster, communication (and miscommunication) is instantaneous. An established alliance that took decades to develop in the previous millennium, might already be ripe and ready for formation today. It depends on the circumstances that surround it, and the propellant the fuels it.

The following are an exploration of potential catalysts that could, in certain circumstances, compel Western nations and Russia to reconsider their positions. Such a shift would likely stem from a convergence of multifaceted crises, shared security threats, and pressing economic necessity.

Economic crisis and shared external threats

One driver for a radical realignment could be the onset of a severe economic crisis. For example, protracted recessions, spiralling inflation, or abrupt disruptions in global trade might force Western countries to reassess their strategic priorities. Internal governing/political weaknesses could make policymakers more open to exploring alternative alliances that provide economic relief or stability. The earlier example of a temptation to move closer to a China-Australia trade agreement, following a surprise tariff hike by a trusted trade partner illustrates this point.

A dramatic escalation in global tensions or the emergence of a common adversary might foster an environment in which the traditional US-led order is perceived as a destabilising rather than a unifying force. In these instances, shared external threats could become the impetus for reconciling differences with Russia, even if temporarily. The purpose would be to achieve a higher achievement of geopolitical stability.

Energy dependency and resource requirements

Energy remains a critical level in international diplomacy. A realignment of trade relationships might be sparked by shifts in global energy dependency. Following the Russian invasion of Ukraine, many Western nations have strived to diversify their energy sources away from Russian supplies. However, should the alternative sources for energy prove inadequate, or energy markets become increasingly volatile, the pragmatic need for reliable energy could push some regions of the West towards reengaging with Russia. Securing energy and raw materials is as crucial to national security as possessing military might. In this scenario, a pathway towards a shift in ideology, based on the need for immediate economic survival and resource stability is possible.

Ceasefire negotiations and diplomatic reconciliation

The possibility of reconciliation of adversaries might emerge from a proactive diplomatic discussion. In a recent example, Ukraine reached a preliminary agreement with the United States to jointly develop its natural resources, including rare earth minerals, oil, and gas, as part of efforts to strengthen economic ties amid ongoing geopolitical tensions. The negotiations, which are still underway as I write this section of the book, were initiated by US President Donald Trump, to secure trade advantage in exchange for Ukraine continuing to receive the military aid established by the previous Biden presidential administration, which has been crucial to Ukraine's ability to defend itself against Russia.

Interestingly, the negotiations have the potential to impact the Australian expert to rare earth minerals to the US, which is exactly what China was proposing as an alternative in the earlier example. Should the US-Ukraine agreement infringe on the US-Australia agreement, there is a possibility for Australia to rethink China's proposal. This scenario also provides an example within the prophecy of how Oceania could begin to align itself to China, if it believes its preexisting alliance to the United States is deteriorating.

Whilst they remain hypothetical examples of triggers that could initiate a shift in global alliances, examples of possible triggers already exist within these examples. All it takes is the right trigger at the right time with the right nation, and a domino effect could be sparked that sweeps across multiple nations.

The Downstairs Neighbour

As NATO is the linchpin, the United States is the safety-pin of a grenade. The linchpin secures together the many moving parts of a bigger mechanism. The safety-pin prevents a grenade from exploding. Since the end of World War Two, the international order, shaping alliances and rule-setting of global engagements has been led by the United States. The US leadership role was underpinned by its military might and economic power, but even more so, by its commitment to a multilateral system of governance.

Recently, the US domestic political turbulence, and the inconsistency of its foreign relations policy has created an unpredictability that is being felt across the world. This uncertainty creates openings for rival powers to contest or even override established alliances. Since the 9/11 terrorist attacks, and increasingly in the past 10 years, the continuous recalibration of US domestic and international policy has sent powerful signals across the world, that the US commitment to stability is over and it's time to rethink the way forward.

In Chapter Seven I discussed the intense polarisation of the American people, politically and culturally. Deep partisan divisions have led to starkly contrasting visions for the United States's role on the world stage. It goes even further, with menacing internal voices, pitting men against women, Black against Hispanic, Christians against Jews, rich against poor, White against Black, Jews against Muslims. Almost every identifying feature of an individual is being weaponised against them in some form, whether it be based on appearance, culture and belief system, gender orientation or socio-economic standing.

For example, the rise of populist or nationalist sentiments, exacerbated by rhetoric on all sides of the political spectrum, has driven policies designed to "win" in the eyes of opinion show audiences, rather than to solve important problems. The United States has also been straying far from long-held traditions and Constitutional norms. For example, as I am writing this, the Trump Administration has failed to act on a unanimous decision by the US Supreme Court, to facilitate the return of a lawful US Resident who was mistakenly deported to El Salvadore.

The US is no longer acting like a committed democracy, that abides by its own Constitution and reliably affords the rights and freedoms of its Constitution to its population of lawful residents and citizens. When the trusted leader of democracy can no longer be trusted to lead by example, even if as a merely a public gesture, there is less of an incentive for other nations to aspire to align to the US principles of democratically aligned world order. Some traditionally Western allies may even feel compelled to recalibrate their own policies, possibly even reassessing their stances towards adversaries, such as the various existing or emerging authoritarian nations, like Russia, China, Saudi Arabia, Iran, and North Korea.

Since Donald Trump assumed his Presidency for the second time this year, discussions have begun to take shape that highlight his interest in shifting the geopolitical landscape. US annexation of Canada, "purchasing" Greenland, and other unorthodox public statements by the President of the United States, are signs that US leadership is fundamentally transforming.

When traditional pillars of the US-led world order start to waver, it undermines confidence and encourages rivals. It brings to the surface a real possibility of fragmentation of the world that will eventually require a comprehensive realignment of global security and economic partnerships.

Ultimately, the United States is potentially the driver and the disruptor of international stability. As its internal divisions spread like a virus until they seep out into the wider world, and its conduct is projected outward to be witnessed by the entire world, everything from global trade, security arrangements and diplomatic engagements are being impacted. Arguably, every nation is recalibrating itself to buffer a US-led incident.

To simplify the complexities of what is likely to be happening inside governmental policy discussions all over the world, we return to the famous saying by Canadian author and social activist Pierre Berton. When a family realises that a crack house has moved in next door, the very next discussion at the dinner table is likely to be whether to put the house up for sale. Could similar discussions be taking place in cabinet meetings of allied nations around the world?

Standing alone

Consider the way that people generally respond to someone who possesses an undeniable presence of confidence, power and self-control. We often feel drawn to people who possess these qualities. Someone who emits a steadying, paternal energy will begin to earn our trust. He might articulate grand gestures, referring to justice, leadership and the protection of those around him. He may give us a sense that he is the steady hand to hold, a person from which we can seek guidance. As time progresses, he becomes someone we can count on to be there when we need him. For years, this person may be the one we trust, the one who can be relied upon when uncertainty looms. We plan around this comforting sense of steadiness. We invite this person into our lives and confide in him our secrets. We feel safe. But then, something shifts.

It starts subtly. Small contradictions in his words, erratic behaviour, choices that don't quite make sense. Sometimes he seems committed to his relationships, promising loyalty, collaboration and shared goals. Then, just as quickly, he pulls away, abandoning commitments, picking fights where none are necessary, leaving people confused about where they stand with him. The unpredictability becomes a pattern of behaviour.

The environment surrounding this person grows uneasy. Some people try to rationalise his actions, convincing themselves that the instability is temporary, that beneath the volatility there is still the same reliable force they had always known. Others start to keep their distance, wary of his unpredictability. Trust, once solid and unquestioned, begins to erode. One by one, we begin to wonder whether relying on him is worth the risk. Perhaps it's time to forge new relationships elsewhere, with people who seem more stable than this person. This chaotic person.

As we each withdraw, this person offers gestures of reconciliation to us. He assures us that the turmoil is behind him, or inadvertent, or someone else's fault. He makes promises, but those promises prove fleeting, overshadowed by the next abruption and disruption, and reversal. The most consistent thing about this person becomes his inconsistency. It creates ongoing doubt and uncertainty, until ultimately a quiet withdrawal of those who had once stood resolutely by his side is complete. He stands alone, a chaos to only himself.

The prophecy predicts a similar shift in alliances as would naturally occur with any interpersonal relationship. Alliances shift, not suddenly, but gradually. Instability replaces confidence, as people begin to prioritise security over sentimentality. The shift is not a rejection of change. The world would not reject the United States, simply because it has changed. The world would shy away from the uncertainty that the destabilisation of the US represents, and the effects of that instability on those other nations.

And regardless of how it may stockpile its own military resources, the distance between a single nation and the unwavering loyalty it once had but has since lost, would be more dangerous than any direct confrontation. Should the United States experience a similar fate, in which its longstanding allies and democratically inspired followers begin to shy away, it will no longer have the power to lead a world that has stopped listening to its confusing and contradictory messages.

Chapter Ten
The Final Shift

> *Until the world, as it is known, will be replaced with the New World. And the New World will last beyond the next millennium.*

This final section of the prophecy is the simplest to understand. It links the prophecy directly to the Bible's Book of Revelation. However, there may be different ways to interpret the outcome of the prophecy, and indeed Revelation, depending on what is meant by "the New World", and other biblical timeline events that must occur to allow the new Millennium to begin.

The Fall of the Final Empire

This book's underlying premise is to discuss a prophecy which focuses itself on the United States, as the "ground zero" location to which all other events leading to a new world order are deferent. As such, the entire book has relevance to the US, even where it speaks about European prophecies. Earlier sections in this chapter have provided prophecy context, to demonstrate how medieval and even more contemporary prophetic claims have originated as Eurocentric but have become aligned to the United States over time. Is this because of the power of the US in the historical snapshot of today? Or is it because of something profoundly bigger that was predicted a long time ago?

It is impossible to begin to discuss the wider concept of how the United States features in prophecy, without acknowledging biblical prophecies. Numerous interpretations of the Bible suggest that the United States plays a role in the "End Times" predictions. The emergence of the US as a global power is believed by many to have been symbolised by the "eagle" referenced in the Book of Revelation 12:13-17, or as the "beast rising from the earth" in Revelation 13:11-18. As discussed in Chapter Eight, predictions by figures such as Nostradamus and Baba Vanga have been aligned to the United States using retrofitted events such as natural disasters and political upheavals, which has added a sense of credibility to biblical prophecy.

In summary, and by no means acting as a precise description of prophetic events, some interpretations of biblical prophecy, for example in the books of Daniel, Matthew and Revelation, describe a turn of events linking the US to "the end of the age". Alternatively, the phrase "end of the world" is used.

The general storyline around this narrative is that Jesus speaks to His disciples about the destruction of the Temple and the signs of the end times. Before this, Jewish history had already witnessed the fall of the First Temple, built by Solomon, which was destroyed by the Babylonians in 586 BC, marking a period of great devastation and exile. Later, Jesus foretells that the magnificent Temple in Jerusalem will be demolished with "not one stone left upon another". This prophecy would later align with the Roman destruction of the (Second) Temple in 70 AD.

Jesus goes on to describe a series of events that will precede the end times, including wars, famines, earthquakes, false prophets and increased wickedness. He emphasises the importance of vigilance and faith, cautioning that no one knows the exact day or hour of the end, "not even the angels in heaven". He also encourages his followers to remain prepared and steadfast in their beliefs.

The narrative links to two similar but slightly misaligned perspectives about the building of the Third and final Temple. In Jewish eschatology, the Third Temple is expected to be built in Jerusalem on the Temple Mount, where the First and Second Temples once stood. It is seen as a place of divine presence and worship, ushering in messianic times during which a new messiah will restore Israel and bring peace to the Earth.

Common Christian interpretations view the Third Temple as an essential element in the end times. It is often linked to the fulfilment of prophecies concerning the return of Jesus Christ.

The Third Temple's construction is relevant to multiple faiths in ways that may appear minor to some but are likely to be paramount to those faiths. It is therefore likely to involve significant political and religious complexity. Whilst there is no specific "empire" foretold to take responsibility for its construction, theological discussions about the building of the Third Temple often include inference relating to Israel, the United States, their relationship to one another and to perceived enemies and adversaries.

Key to the predictions surrounding the Third Temple and "end times", "end of the age", or "end of the world", depending on source, are two distinct figures.

To adequately describe the relevance of the United States as a final empire, signifying the return or revival of Israel, and how biblical prophecy aligns as a larger, umbrella prophecy to which the prophecy examined in this book is position within, would require an entirely separate book. However, the prophecy I encountered in the 1980s certainly appears to align with the wider biblical framework. This is hardly surprising given that the prophecy I saw had been written by a religious organisation, despite my failure to confirm which religion.

Book of Revelation Prophecy

Christianity speaks to the idea of ultimate accountability. A fundamental principle of Christian religious belief centres around the premise that every action and decision matters in the grand scheme of life. It highlights the contrast between redemption and separation, sparking discussions about moral responsibility, the nature of justice, and the finality of consequences.

In the Christian interpretation, spiritual warfare between good and evil ultimately leads to humanity's salvation, involving a Millennium of

Peace, a brief period of rebellion, and a final battle after which an eternal salvation occurs.

Pre-Millennium period

Ezekiel 40-48 details a vision of a future temple which has been long interpreted as referring to a Third physical Temple in Jerusalem. Daniel 9:27 speaks of a covenant being made and later broken, which some ascribe to the existence of ceremonial practices and rituals (temple rites) that must be breached during the period referred to as the "End of Days" – another way to describe the end times. For the religious interpretation of the Millennium of Peace to occur, the pre-Millennium Third Temple must be built and established as a place of worship.

Returning to Daniel 9:27, the breaking of the covenant relates to a time when a deceptive leader will undermine true worship. This leader is commonly interpreted to be the Antichrist. 2Thessalonians 2:4 describes a "man of sin" who exalts himself. This suggests that the emergence of a powerful deceiver challenges divine authority. The context within which this occurs assumes the Antichrist character to be a charismatic, globally influential leader who deceives nations. He initially presents himself to be a bringer of peace but later betrays those who believed him by imposing oppression and demanding to be worshipped. The verse appears as follows:

> *"Who opposeth and exalteth himself above all that is called God, or that is worshipped; so that he as God sitteth in the temple of God, shewing himself that he is God."*

The Great Tribulation and the battle preparations occur in the next biblical phase. This is an era marked by intense suffering, deception and widespread conflict. Worshippers and true believers face harsh persecution. The global unrest and spiritual deception during this period prepare the world for an ultimate, climactic confrontation between good and evil.

Towards the end of the tribulation, the forces of evil, rallied by the Antichrist and inspired by Satan, gather for a decisive battle in a place referred to in Hebrew as Armageddon. Revelation 16-19 describe a detailed account of the savage confrontation of good versus evil, and how it sets the stage for Christ's return and the subsequent divine intervention that ushers in the new Millennium.

The Millennium and its aftermath

Revelation 20 describes the events that occur to commencing the new Millennium. In verses 1-3, an angel descends from Heaven with a key to what is referred to as the bottomless pit. He binds Satan and casts him into the pit, thus confining Satan for one thousand years (the New Millennium). During this time, Christ rules the world, ensuring peace and righteousness. The souls of those who were killed, or who otherwise resisted the Mark of the Beast, are resurrected. They are early to live in eternity with Christ and are safeguarded from a subsequent "final battle" (Verses 4-6).

Verses 7-8 speak of the release of Satan from his prison in the bottomless pit, at the end of the thousand-year period. He has not learned his lesson and quickly mobilises the world's nations in vast numbers for the final battle. The aim is to deceive the world one last time, as a final test for Humanity.

The remainder of Chapter 20 speaks of the Final Judgement. As the forces of evil surround a "beloved city" widely believed by religious scholars to be Jerusalem, fire comes down from Heaven to devour the evil forces. Satan is ultimately cast into a lake of fire. This marks the end of Satan, inferring that no new evil can occur following his demise.

All remaining souls are subsequently resurrected in verses 10-15 and stand before God in an act of Final Judgement. Books, recording the deeds of every person who ever lived are opened and each person is judged according to how they lived their life. Revelation 20 does claim that certain people will not have their names entered into the books, which is an omission that will prevent them from being included in God's final salvation of Humanity. Instead, they will be subject to a "second death" in which their souls will be destroyed forever.

This conclusive phase brings about the final separation between good and evil. It represents accountability and marks the end of the cosmic struggle that has been taking place. The struggle itself is believed to have endured since the creation of the Heaven and the Earth, millions of years ago. However, the Bible is not specific about this.

The remainder of the Bible (Revelation 21 and 22) provide an intriguing and seemingly unnecessary explanation of how the Heaven and Earth that has existed since first mention in Genesis 1, are subsequently replaced by "a new Heaven and a new Earth" (Revelation 21:1), during which there will be an entirely different type of reality. Interpretations of this new Heaven and Earth are beyond the scope of this book but warrant consideration in the context of other interpretations in this chapter.

I do not want to overshadow the message of the prophecy to which this book is specific to by over-analysing every aspect of the wider End Times Prophecy. However, there are certain aspects of biblical prophecy that are uncannily familiar in this current time. I refer in this regard to the Antichrist and the Mark of the Beast.

Who or what is the Antichrist?

In Christian eschatology, particularly based on the Book of Revelation, the Antichrist is a figure who opposes Christ and deceives the world. Some interpretations suggest that the Antichrist may use the Third Temple to claim divine authority or enact deception.

The False Prophet, often considered a partner of the Antichrist, is described as leading people to worship the Antichrist. The False Prophet is also attributed to the introduction of a "mark of the beast", and to performing signs to deceive believers. Both the Antichrist and False Prophet are central to narratives of the end times and the trials faced by Humanity before divine judgement.

While Christians believe the Antichrist to be a person, there is the alternative possibility that any person who meets the biblical criteria of Antichrist, may in fact simply be someone who gives strength to an antichrist element. In this instance, a person possessing antichrist characteristics may be conflated with anti-Christlike outcomes that push the End Times timeline forward.

The Antichrist as a human figure

The various interpretation of the Antichrist as a figure come from passages in both the Old and New Testaments of the Bible. Depending on which passages are relied upon, the Antichrist can differ slightly. Just as God and Jesus are assumed to have many different names in the Bible, so does the Antichrist. Depending on which names are attributed to him, more and more characteristics can be adopted.

Some of the names used to describe the Antichrist include "the promise that shall come; a fierce king; a master of intrigue; a despicable man; a worthless shepherd; the one who brings destruction; the lawless one; the evil man, and the beast".

The key thing to note about the Antichrist is that he is anti-Christ. Christ, particularly in the New Testament, is seen as the embodiment of love. If Christ is love in the New Testament, then the anti of love is the Antichrist. More specifically, the anti of love, and therefore the anti of Christ, is described in biblical detail. An exploration of some of the most significant passages in the Bible about the Antichrist bring up a rather clear image of the type of man who may fit the criteria. It narrows the pool of possible candidates significantly.

The Antichrist is a figure who is against or opposed to Christ, opposed to love. The term "anti" can also mean *instead of*. In this context, the Antichrist is a figure who will pretend to be Christ or who will be content to be mistaken for or assumed to be Christ.

The Antichrist is also someone who may reject love. This can be seen in two different ways: either the Antichrist rejects love by existing in a manner that seemingly opposes the way of love; or they reject the idea that love, and therefore Christ, exists.

The Antichrist is referenced many times as being associated with falsehoods and blasphemy. He boasts a lot about himself, speaking arrogant words against others in power. He requires that people worship him. He will also be ruthless, without compassion towards others. As a result, he will persecute, torture and kill people while he is in power. According to the Bible, the Antichrist is in power for 42 months. However, the description of what is meant by the word "power" isn't clarified. Does this mean he will hold a position of power for that duration of time? Will he simply give a practical display of power during that period? There is a difference between having the title of someone who is powerful and exerting a powerful influence over others. Many a powerful people exist in the shadows of society and are routinely unidentified as being without controlling power.

Moving on to specific Bible verses, John 4:3 states that "every spirit that does not confess Jesus is not from God", and that "this is the spirit of the Antichrist". John 2:18 says "just as you heard that Antichrist is coming, even now many Antichrists have appeared". Similarly, 2 John 1:7 states that "many deceivers have gone out into the world, those who do not acknowledge Jesus Christ as coming in the flesh". These passages emphasize the presence of multiple Antichrists and suggest that rejecting Christ or not confessing Jesus could align a person with the Antichrist's spirit.

Daniel 7:8 states, "While I was contemplating the horns, behold, another horn, a little one, came up among them, and three of the first horns were pulled out by the roots before it; and behold, this horn possessed eyes like the eyes of a man and a mouth uttering great boasts." This passage describes the Antichrist as a boaster, insolent, arrogant, prideful and haughty. Daniel 8:25 says, "he will magnify himself in his heart." Daniel 11:36 says, "he will exalt himself and magnify himself above every god." These passages emphasise the Antichrist's tendency to boast and artificially inflate his self-worth.

Daniel 8;12 says that the Antichrist "will cast truth down to the ground", meaning he will speak many lies and untruths as though the truth no longer exists. Revelation 13:5 says, "And he was given a mouth speaking great things and blasphemies, and he was given authority to continue for forty-two-months". This passage highlights the Antichrist's power to boast and make offensive declarations, as well as the tenure of his position of power.

Matthew 24:24 claims that the Antichrist will be given authority, potentially over a kingdom or nation, for 42 months. This authority is described as significant, though the exact nature of the power dynamic is unclear.

Daniel 11:21 describes the Antichrist as vile. A vile person is indecent, crass, or stoops to low levels that shock people and make them think negatively of him. Terms like morally bad, wicked, despicable, and abhorrent appear in the dictionary as descriptions for "vile." It refers to someone who cannot be trusted to act ethically, takes advantage of others, cheats to get what they want, and may act in revengeful or harsh ways. This description aligns with the perception of a person who offends others to the point of being considered vile.

Daniel 7:20 describes the Antichrist as being "more stout than his fellows." This could indicate physical stature, suggesting that the Antichrist is larger than those around him. However, the word "stout" can also refer to arrogance, implying that the Antichrist is filled with pride and self-importance. Both interpretations provide insight into the characteristics attributed to the Antichrist.

Daniel 8:25 offers a profound description: "And through his policy also he shall cause craft to prosper in his hand; and he shall magnify himself in his heart, and by peace shall destroy many: he shall also stand up against the prince of princes; but he shall be broken without hand." This verse suggests that the Antichrist will use cunning and deceit to achieve his goals, magnify himself with pride and arrogance, and use peace as a deceptive tool to destroy many. The phrase "by peace shall destroy many" implies that the Antichrist may promote peace, but at a cost that leads to destruction.

The verse also states, "He shall also stand up against the prince of princes," implying opposition to God. Finally, the phrase "But he shall be broken without hand" signifies that the Antichrist will not be defeated by human hands but by the act of God.

The Antichrist is also referred to as the "lawless one" in 2Thessalonians 2:8 and 2:9. This title describes an entity who disregards legality and acts without accountability. Despite engaging in lawless behavior, the Antichrist is said to evade punishment, reinforcing the idea of being "broken without hand."

Noone can stop the Antichrist figure, but he will succumb to a divine act. This implies a death by illness, accident, natural end of life, or some type of perceived divine intervention.

The Antichrist as symbol of influence

The most notable ways in which biblical prophecy may be describing the Antichrist as a symbol of influence, rather than a figure, appear in the Book of John, and the references above (4:3, 2:18, 2 1:7). There are other similar types of descriptions of the Antichrist which are widespread throughout the Bible, particularly in the New Testament. However, John arguably contains the most concise collection of clarifying verses.

Despite Christians generally interpreting the Antichrist to be a person, many previous antichrists have lived before. Julius Caesar and Adolph Hitler are often believed to have been earlier antichrist characters. What they have in common may be an antichrist energy, or a combination of personal characteristics that bring out an antichrist response in others.

Christ Consciousness

To understand the influence of antichrist influence, it is necessary to first understand the concept of *Christ Consciousness*.

Christ consciousness is a term that links traditional Christian spirituality to longstanding interpretations of spiritual awakening, some of which date back to far earlier civilisations.

Christianity teaches that Christ consciousness refers not only to following the teachings of Jesus Christ but also to embodying the qualities he exemplified. These qualities include unconditional love, compassion, wisdom, forgiveness, and deep inner peace. Christianity teaches that a Christlike state of awareness resides within everyone, and that by awakening to this higher state, individuals can transcend ego-driven limitations to experience a profound connection with the divine and all of creation.

However, the idea of awakening to a higher state of consciousness, where the innermost self is connected to a greater divine presence, is not unique to Christianity. In fact, long before the historical emergence of Christianity, ancient spiritual traditions were already exploring similar spiritual awakenings.

For instance, Hinduism dates to around 3300 BC. Hinduism centres on the concept of true self (Atman) and the interconnectedness of a universal essence (Brahman). This idea is clearly articulated in texts like the *Upanishads* and the *Bhagavad Gita*, where the quest for self-realization and the dissolution of the ego lead to a state of inner awakening. In *Advaita Vedanta*, a Hindu philosophy, the goal is to realize that there is no essential division between the individual and the divine. This teaching resonates with the idea of Christ consciousness as the awakening of the divine spark within.

Other ancient belief systems, such as early forms of Neoplatonism and Gnosticism, also emphasised the idea of an inner light or divine spark that transcends ordinary dualistic thought when awakened. These traditions taught that through contemplation, mindfulness and transformative practice, a person could access higher wisdom, and alignment with universal love and truth.

Many modern spiritual practitioners, regardless of their religious background, regard the journey toward Christ consciousness as a personal path of inner transformation. Techniques such as meditation, contemplative prayer, mindfulness, and self-reflection are commonly employed to quiet the mind, let go of egoic attachments, and open the heart. The process is often described as awakening to an inner light or the inner divinity within, where one comes to see life and all beings through the lens of unconditional love. In this state, the individual experiences a deep sense of interconnectedness with all life. It becomes a recognition that what they do to others, they do to themselves.

Overall, while the term Christ Consciousness can be traced to the figure of Jesus Christ, it has been called other names and has existed long before the assumed life of Jesus, as an embodiment of spiritual maturity. It calls on the individual to look within, recognize the divine spark present in all beings, and commit to living in a way that reflects the highest ideals of love and truth. This comprehensive understanding encourages both personal growth and a more compassionate global community, suggesting that the transformation of the self can lead to the healing of society.

The concept of Christ as a consciousness - a spiritual aspect of the self - is not new and has even been applied to Jesus himself. Docetism, an early Gnostic Christian belief, held that Christ was a divine spirit who temporarily inhabited Jesus rather than being permanently united with him. In this view, Christ descended upon Jesus at pivotal moments - such as his baptism - but departed before his crucifixion, leaving Jesus to experience suffering and death alone, without the divine presence.

This interpretation suggests that any individual has the potential to ascend or descend into a state that opens them to either Christ-consciousness or antichrist energies, depending on their spiritual receptivity.

When Christ consciousness is described in its simplest form in a modern-day context, it appears to be the awakening to a sense of self and sense of the collective as harmoniously one in the same. This then defines the antichrist as being an influence that destroys the sense of self and divides the collective.

The Antichrist as a series of actions and events

There are numerous events, signs and calamities that will befall the Earth within the timeline of the Antichrist. Natural disasters, cosmic events, unusual sounds and sightings.

There are also specific actions that are attributed to the Antichrist. For example, in John 5:31-47, Jesus explains why people should believe in him. He talks about miracles and written word that demonstrate the authority and mission Jesus has been sent with. Despite these testimonies, many people continue to refuse to believe in Jesus. In John 5:43, Jesus acknowledges this, saying: "I have come in My Father's name, and you do not receive Me; if another comes in his own name, him you will receive."

This verse refers to the Antichrist arriving on the scene promoting his own name as a badge of honour or an aspect to be worshipped, like how God wants people to worship Him.

In the modern-day context, using a name as a badge of honour is referred to as branding. Just as brands like Hoover, Kleenex, or Band-Aid have become household terms, the Antichrist's name could carry an expectation of worship and confidence. This verse highlights the power of branding and its ability to influence people's perceptions and actions.

Next, 2Thessalonians 2:1-5 provides a wealth of insight into the Antichrist:

> *"Now, brethren, concerning the coming of our Lord Jesus Christ and our gathering together to Him, we ask you, not to be soon shaken in mind or troubled, either by spirit or by word or by letter, as if from us, as though the day of Christ had come. Let no one deceive you by any means; for that Day will not come unless the falling away comes first, and the man of sin is revealed, the son of perdition, who opposes and exalts himself above all that is called God or that is worshiped, so that he sits as God in the temple of God, showing himself that he is God."*

This passage warns Christians not to be deceived, explaining that the return of Christ will only occur after the "falling away" and the revelation of the "man of sin", the Antichrist. The Antichrist is described as embracing the seven deadly sins: pride, greed, envy, wrath, sloth, gluttony, and lust. Pride is evident in the Antichrist's boasting and self-exaltation. Greed is reflected in the pursuit of wealth and luxury. Envy manifests in resentment toward others who are more admired or successful. Wrath is seen in anger and vengeful actions. Sloth and gluttony may be present in lethargy and excessive consumption, while lust is associated with immoral desires.

The "falling away" refers to Christians turning away from traditional teachings and following the Antichrist's word. This phenomenon occurs in a divided Christian belief system, where divisions arise between those who prioritize spiritual transcendence and those who adopt a militant approach to their faith. For the latter, the Antichrist is someone who appears like a "Savior" to protect their movement and fight perceived enemies on their behalf. Christians who feel marginalised and under siege turn to a figure who does not observe their etiquette or rules, believing that this gives him the freedom to protect their movement in ways they cannot. This apocalyptic, "barbarians at the gates" mentality fuels the falling away described in 2Thessalonians.

The Book of Micah, chapter 5, verses 2-15 discusses battles between Israel and her enemies, particularly the Assyrians. Some interpretations suggest that the Assyrian reference foreshadows the Antichrist. Micah 5:5 states: "When the Assyrian comes into our land,

and when he treads in our palaces, we will rise against him." However, other passages, such as Isaiah 10:5-12, describe the Assyrian as the rod of God's anger, leading to scholarly debate about whether this refers to the Antichrist or historical enemies of Israel.

The Assyrians referred to in the Bible were part of the ancient Assyrian Empire, which was centred in the region of Mesopotamia. This area corresponds to modern-day northern Iraq, northeastern Syria, southeastern Turkey, and parts of northwestern Iran. The capital cities of the Assyrian Empire, such as Nineveh and Ashur, were located along the Tigris River in what is now Iraq. The section of prophecy discussed in this chapter speaks of the US being attacked by 3 nations. I recalled Russia and China, but there is a 3rd nation that I do not recall. In the context of biblical prophecy and considering the close military relationship between Israel and the United States, the 3rd nation may be Iran, or a coalition of nations near that region.

The Book of Daniel also discusses four beasts, representing four empires that rise and fall. The fourth beast is believed to be the Roman Empire. Daniel 7:7-8 and 23-25 describe this beast and speak of the revival of the Roman Empire, from which the Antichrist will emerge. This revival is sometimes interpreted as the modern-day United States, which shares governing and societal similarities with the Roman Empire.

Daniel 9:26-27 states: "The people of the prince who is to come will destroy the city and the sanctuary." This is a reference to the Roman destruction of Jerusalem around 70 AD, with the "prince to come" considered to be the Antichrist. Revelation 17:9-10 also describes a beast with seven heads, interpreted as a reference to Rome, famously known as the city on seven hills. These passages suggest a connection between the Antichrist and Roman descent. This may be so, but it may equally be referring to another form of beast, which is discussed later in this chapter. Daniel 11:30 describes the Antichrist adorning his home with gold, silver, precious stones, and pleasant things.

Finally, 2Thessalonians 2:7-12 offers a profound description:

> *"The mystery of the lawlessness is already at work. He who now restrains will do so until he has taken out of the way. And then the lawless one will be revealed, whom the Lord will consume with the breath of his mouth and destroy with the brightness of his coming. The coming of the lawless one is according to the working of Satan, with all the power, signs and lying wonders, and with all unrighteous deception among those who perish, because they did not receive the love of the truth, that they might be saved. And for this reason, God will send them strong delusion, that they should believe the lie. That they all may be condemned who did not believe the truth but had pleasure in the unrighteousness."*

This passage emphasizes the Antichrist's lawlessness, deception, and reliance on Satan's power, as well as a delusion sent by God and referred to as "the lie". Those who have fallen away from the traditional Christian faith, will be deceived by the lie and will take pleasure in the cognitive awareness that they are aligning to an unrighteousness.

The Rise of the Beast

As previously mentioned, Revelation 17:9-10 describes a beast with seven heads, interpreted as a reference to Rome. The interpretation dates to early Christian writings. The imagery of the "seven mountains" described in scripture was attributed to Rome, in light of it having been built on seven hills. This connection was recognised by early Church Fathers, such as Tertullian (155-240 AD) and Augustine of Hippo (354-430 AD), who interpreted the passage as a reference to Rome's political and spiritual influence.

However, the association of the *Beast of Rome* was particularly relevant during the Roman Empire's dominance, as Christians face persecution under Roman rule. The symbolism of the beast and its seven heads was seen as a critique of the Empire's power and idolatry. Over time, this interpretation became a cornerstone of eschatological thought, influencing discussions about the end times and the role of Rome in biblical prophecy.

An interpretation during the periods of Tertullian and Augustine of Hippo could not have anticipated the starkly different world that would be commonplace during the end of days. The way of life, the degree of scientific and technological advancement that has occurred since the early Christian period would have been unthinkable back then. It is therefore likely that the 7 heads of the beast was a reference, not to Rome, but to something else.

Is it possible that we are witnessing the beast's rise today?

The Magnificent Race

At the time of writing this book, there are 7 globally recognised technology giants: Apple, Meta (formerly known as Facebook), Microsoft, NVIDIA, Tesla, Alphabet (Google), and Amazon. Collectively, they dominate industries across a broad technological spectrum and are the driving force for innovation. As such, they are referred to as "The Magnificent Seven".

A global race to develop artificial intelligence (AI) is presently underway. It is the defining competition for technology. There is no parallel. The world's biggest corporations, along with its richest nations, are investing billions to secure AI technology breakthroughs that promise not only economic superiority but also transformative societal change.

The Magnificent Seven has emerged as the private sector leaders of AI innovation. Each plays a unique role in the AI development ecosystem. Collectively, these technology giants are reshaping the geopolitical and economic systems of the world. In fact, despite being only 7 publicly traded companies, they represent approximately 35 percent of the 500 largest publicly traded companies in the United States. This translates to around 16% of the global stock market.

The race to harness AI's potential has left the Magnificent Seven to race, largely under-regulated, answering primarily to shareholders who are cheering them on. There are regulations in place for AI development, predominantly based on pre-existing protections of data protection, consumer rights and anti-discrimination. However, the pace of development is exponential, whereas government legislation is lethargic and littered with political minefields.

AI that is directly accessed by the public is generally done so in the online space. As it happens, the online space is also under-regulated. Every day, people feed information into a developing, insatiable system.

There are benefits to continuing the hot pursuit of AI advancement, coupled with serious concerns about how it may impact Humanity. The arguments in favour include the prospects of AI enhancing human capabilities, the opportunities for economic and social advancement, unforeseeable scientific and technological breakthroughs, and global competitiveness and ongoing innovation.

Cause for Concern

One of the most significant concerns about AI centres on the ambitions of merging technology and biology. Cybernetic systems, brain-computer interfaces, and neural implants are all in development and becoming more sophisticated each day. This gives rise to deep concerns about whether humanity may begin to see a fundamental shift in which it means to be human. The worry is that by integrating AI directly into our biological systems, we might alter cognitive processes in unpredictable ways. The risks include the reshaping the "human experience", destroying the ability to think subjectively, and challenging the existence of personal identity.

The fusion of technology and biology also raises ethical questions about privacy, autonomy and the potential for inadvertently creating a new way to separate people. If some people have access to neuro-enhancement and other do not, will this deepen and already deep social divide? Unintended consequences may not be foreseeable, leading to behaviours and thoughts that are not fully understood within the current societal framework. One of the consequences has already been discussed in this book. The consequence of diminishing the human sense of self-worth as outlined in Maslow's Hierarchy of Needs pyramid. Stunting the nullifying the cognitive value of humanity.

The biggest question is whether we will continue to be human if we allow technology to integrate with the human consciousness? And considering prophecy, particularly biblical prophecy, is human consciousness in fact Christ Consciousness?

Furthermore, is the technological race to develop AI coinciding with prophetic warnings of a beast aligned with an antichrist factor that redefines Humanity, and thereby threatens to destroy us? There is a growing population of individuals, from all areas of science, business, education and philosophy who are warning that every person alive now is at risk of transhumanism, at a time when people are being "pitted against people" and "against ourselves", teaching younger generations to defer to technology, automatically accept artificial enhancements, and to believe their natural selves to be inferior to those enhancements. In some cases, the warning includes predictions that the present humans on Earth, may be some of the last, if the current trajectory is left to continue.

On this point, the prophecy that I read in the 1980s, alongside the wider biblical Ends Times Prophecy, appear to give credence to this warning.

Interwoven Forces deciding our Fate?

Depending on where a person searches, they will find a continuous discussion taking place relating to duality of life. Whether philosophy, spirituality, psychology or science, each revolves around the concept of dual forces, interwoven into reality as we know it.

The key theories and interpretations regarding duality and its relation to reality, are all relevant to the messages contained within the prophecy examined herein. The explanations and nuances may differ, but the context is always the same. There is more than one, but only one can prevail to move forward.

Philosophical debate regarding dualism or monism

At its heart, dualism is the idea that reality is composed of two distinct kinds of substance or principle. The French mathematician, natural scientist and philosopher, René Descartes (1596-1650 AD) advanced the notion that spiritual mind (soul) and physical body are fundamentally different things that interact with one another. This approach highlights a tension between mental phenomena, involving thoughts or consciousness, and the material aspects of life. It suggests that opposites coexist, namely spirit and matter, and they exist side by side but separate to one another.

In contrast, monism contends that only one kind of substance underlies all of reality. Whether the single substance is considered in a material and physical sense, or spiritually within the context of idealism, the proposal is that we perceive a variety of aspects of the only single whole thing that exists.

Whilst this physiological interpretation of monism isn't based on spiritual belief systems, it does coincide with the early Christian teachings of Gnosticism, or even earlier belief systems such as the mystical Kabbalistic faith. Both belief systems teach that seemingly opposing forces exist simultaneously and interdependently. Writings from both speak of light and darkness coexisting within the human soul and in the divine emanations. The dual aspects (such as "light" and "darkness" within a person) are interwoven. They are combined facets of one ultimate reality that need each other to exist. The idea is less about strict opposition and more about a dynamic balance that, when fully integrated, reveals the underlying unity of all existence.

In mathematics, a similar principle exists. Albert Einstein's famous equation, $E=mc^2$, is a mathematical representation of the principle of mass-energy equivalence. The purpose of the equation is to demonstrate the coexistence of independent forces that can be interchanged with one another. The letter E stands for energy, the letter m stands for mass, and the c^2 is a constant representation for the speed of light. The equation tells us that a small amount of mass can be converted into a tremendous amount of energy, and vice versa, because the speed of light squared makes it possible.

In other words, mass is energy and energy is mass, depending on the factor of light speed.

West v. East Philosophies

In Christianity, duality is often expressed as the ongoing conflict between good and evil, light and darkness, sin and redemption. This duality underpins narratives of falling away from God, and salvation. It frames the human struggle within a moral and cosmic order of existence. For example, the ultimate victory over evil that appears in the Book of Revelation is considered in Christian teachings to be a final resolution of this cosmic conflict.

In Eastern thought, including traditions like Taoism and Hinduism, the opposition of competing forces, such as light and dark, or passive and active, are interdependent and complementary. Each is dependent upon the other and cannot exist without the other also existing. Eastern philosophies teach that the separateness that we perceive is a temporary illusion that is constructed by the mind.

Psychological perspectives

The works of the psychologist, Carl Jung are fundamental to discussions of duality in the context of the inner self. Jung introduced the concept of everything existing alongside a "shadow" aspect of itself, representing the unconscious and often repressed side of reality, particularly within a human personality. Stemming from this theory, modern psychological theories also suggest that recognising and reconciling duality helps to build resilience and a deeper understanding of motivations and behaviours.

Scientific and Cosmological duality

Quantum mechanics is where the most striking examples of duality in science can be found. The phenomenon where elementary particles behave differently depending on whether they are being visually observed at the time.

In some experiments, they spread out and appear in wave-like formation, creating patterns like ripples on water, while in other experiments, they appear as individual, localized particles. This dual behavior shows that at the quantum level nature doesn't fit neatly into our everyday categories of "particle" or "wave".

The Old gives way to the New

These varying perspectives are each based on approaches and beliefs that are generally considered to be contradictory. Is the scientific perspective the only accuracy? Is spirituality the way? What is the truth? Examining these viewpoints reveals that duality is not merely a feature of life, but a framework through which we can understand the richly layered and sometimes paradoxical nature of our reality.

The Bible predicts a shift from Old to New Worlds. When interpreted through the religious realm of darkness and light, good and evil, the Bible reads like a physical battle that must take place to cleanse the world of satanic forces that seem to have no purpose other than to torturously and endlessly test Humanity's resolve.

However, when examined in light of the prophecy I encountered in the 1980s, a modern roadmap of how we arrived in this crossroads environment begins to take place.

Somehow, the future was foretold through prophecy. This thought will be expanded in the next chapter. The unfathomable way a small booklet from 40 years ago, or a large book from 2000 years ago, could predict the current day with the specificity acknowledged in this book is one thing. The other thing, however, is that both the small and large books place us at a crossroad between two aspects of duality. The past reveals the future. Light competes with dark. Good battles evil. The old makes way for the new. But why?

The prophecy discussed in this book, just like the Bible's End Times prophecy, serves a purpose. It has an intention, which is why it was presented for consumption and consideration. As explained at the commencement of this book, my examination of this prophecy seems to reveal that we are being given fair warning of what is to come, so that we can either prepare for, prevent, or hold at bay, the events foretold. There are a range of possibilities as to which interpretations of prophecy, life and reality are accurate. There is also a possibility that all interpretations are a piece in the puzzle of accuracy.

Either way, after 40 years of trying to understand, I do believe that there is sufficient evidence within this book to show that we are existing within a scripted reality. The next chapter examines the various possibilities of why such a scripted reality may be unfolding, its purpose, and how we are being given a chance to control the future of Humanity.

Chapter Eleven
Revelation

During a 4-year period, I encountered a series of dreams that I publicly and contemporaneously discussed with thousands of people around the world. I am the host of a social media platform called *Ellie Dreams Down Under* which was named as such to reflect the variety of peculiar dreams that, converging with the 1980s prophecy, thrust me into a public-facing role in the first place.

Over the years, my continuing interest in the predictions of the prophecy, new information I found through research, and my exploration of esoteric, spiritual and religious matters, have combined with my dreams to reveal a central theme. There are clues as to what the purpose of foretelling through prophecy might be. There are clues as to what Humanity can do about these clues. We can control our collective future. I believe that wholeheartedly, and a primary reason why I'm writing this book is to help others to see what I have come to believe I can see.

Everything is a clue, a piece in the puzzle of what it means to live in a reality that was scripted thousands of years ago. The script of our reality was shared with us for a reason. We are meant to identify the clues, decipher them, and spread the word of them to others, so that the collective spirit can use the clues as stepping stones on a path of our own choosing.

Kamala Harris and the Scarf

On 11 March 2020, at the Democratic Primary debate between Joe Biden and Bernie Sanders, Mr Biden announced that he would be choosing a female vice-presidential running mate.

2020 US Presidential Election

One night in July 2020 I had a 2-part dream about some of the women who were being discussed by the media as candidates for the vice-presidential role. In the first part of the dream, I was made aware of a colourful silk-like scarf, fluttering in a light breeze. The scene was taking place outside, but I was unable to see anything notable, except the scarf, and an old document that looked as though it might be an antique opened scroll. The document contained faded lettering, in a font like Old English Text. I didn't focus on what was written as the scarf's vibrant colours and patterns had caught my attention.

In the dream, I was aware that there were many people present, despite not being able to see any people. I could also hear a soft rustling sound, like random movements that were taking place around me. It seemed that I was dreaming of an important moment, defined by the scroll and the scarf.

The scarf contained a unique pattern that I'd never seen before. It was comprised of diagonal segments of colour. There were 3 different, alternating segments. The first was a red, white and blue. reminiscent of the US flag. It comprised stars and stripes in odd formation. The second was a bold yellow segment, unpatterned.

The third was a glorious segment of many colourful flowers that reminded me of a blouse my mother had once sewn for herself many years ago. She used to wear the blouse often, and every time I saw it, a thought always crossed my mind about how bright and bold the colours of the flowers were, but with a lovely soft hue that added a pleasant elegance to the design. The 3 different diagonals repeated along the length of the scarf.

I woke up with the memory of this dream and remained awake for a few minutes. I got up from bed and visited the powder room, after which I returned to bed and promptly fell back to sleep.

I subsequently recall having a second dream that appeared as a continuation of the first. In this dream a parade of the known vice-presidential candidates was trying on the scarf from my previous dream. The first candidate I recall was Stacey Abrams, a political activist lawyer from the US State of Georgia. I had dreamt of Ms Abrams a few weeks earlier and recalled that she had been referred to as a "stringer" in my dream – a word I later had to look up in the dictionary to understand its meaning. The term "stringer" is used to describe a reporter who is assigned a specific location from which to report the news. They are a local correspondent, focusing on the news issues of that location. Ms Abrams had appeared in the dream in a *Jessica Rabbit* type of persona. Standing in a kitchen, flanked by 2 rival men, who were vying for her attention. She acknowledged neither and instead smiled at me in a way that I would expect *Ms Rabbit* to do. One of the men called her a stringer, and then I woke up.

In the scarf dream, Ms Abrams looked uncomfortable, as though the scarf didn't fit her properly. She tugged at it and looked as though she didn't want to wear it.

The next person to try the scarf was Val Demings, a Florida Democrat who had served as one of the Impeachment Managers during the first impeachment of Donald Trump. I recall that the scarf was indefinably wrong for Ms Demings. I watched her pass slowly by in my dream, and the scarf had no impact on me. It seemed bland.

The third person to appear in my view wearing the scarf was Elizabeth Warren, a Democrat Senator from Massachusetts. Seeing Ms Warren in the scarf was jarring. The colours did not suit her at all, and the yellow segments of the scarf directly seemed to conflict with her skin tone. I remember thinking to myself as I was dreaming "Oh, Elizabeth, yellow is definitely not your colour!"

The final candidate to enter view, as though on a slow-moving conveyor belt, was Kamala Harris, a Democratic Senator from California. Ms Harris was wearing the scarf, and immediately she brought the colours of the scarf to life. In my dream, it seemed that the scarf was specifically made for her to wear. There was a sense of excitement, vibrancy, and joyousness to the ensemble. The colours and fabric fibres seemed perfect, and Ms Harris looked happy, verging on triumphant.

I woke up from this second dream, instantly knowing that Ms Harris would be the individual chosen for the job. I told many people about my dreams, including family and online audiences. I had also told people of my Stacey Abrams dream, and together these dreams seemed to indicate that Ms Abrams would remain focused on grassroots issues in Georgia, while Ms Harris would appear in front of the US Constitution, depicted by the antique scroll of my dream, at the Presidential Inaugural Ceremony.

2024 US Presidential Election

Four years after this 2-part dream, in the week prior to the 2024 Presidential Election, I dreamt that I was hovering above a skirmish taking place between 2 massive umbrellas. Beneath the umbrellas were opposing groups of people, the combined sum of which was massive, thousands or even millions.

Between the 2 umbrellas was what appeared to be long sticks, resembling chopsticks. They were tied together with something that I couldn't immediately identify. The energy of the debates and fighting was causing the sticks to rock like a pendulum, back and forth, increasing in speed and intensity until they were swinging wildly from side to side, umbrella to umbrella.

There came a moment as I approached from above the scene, that the sticks swung so sharply that they lost their grounding and flew erratically into the air. The force of their escape was sufficient to loosen the grip of the item that had been binding them together. It began to unravel in the wild wind. As it unfolded and began to fly solo, I recognised it as the scarf that had suited Kamala Harris so well as Vice-Presidential Candidate, four years earlier.

The dream was incredibly vivid, in colour and emotional impact. I woke up feeling as though I'd simultaneously suffered extreme losses and celebrated major wins at a sporting event. The feelings were quite overwhelming, but they were a mishmash. I couldn't tell what my excitement represented. Happiness? Anger? General anxiety?

I told everyone I encountered in the following few days about my dream. I tried to decipher the dream to see if I could figure out its meaning. I decided upon the idea that the umbrellas represented Left vs. Right issues in the United States, and that the release of the scarf that ultimately flew above it all, was an acknowledgement that Kamala Harris, the Democratic Presidential Candidate in the upcoming election, was going to win.

It turns out that I was right about the dream. It was predicting the outcome of the US Presidential Election. However, it was doing more than that. It was predicting the immediate future of the United States, as foretold by the prophecy I encountered in my youth.

It took me a few months to decipher the symbolism of my dreams about the colourful scarf that had occurred 4 years apart, and how those dreams interplayed with one another. Gradually, I began to see that the earlier dream had positioned Kamala Harris to be a representative figure for US democracy. The later dream demonstrated how she may have been able to hold a country together that was enmeshed in a longstanding skirmish of miscellaneous grievances and divisive ideologies.

The bound sticks represented divisive issues that had swelled into towering monoliths of conflict. They loomed over the people with such formidable weight that resolution seemed an insurmountable task, casting shadows of doubt on all who stood beneath them. The silk scarf that bound the sticks together was the silk thread linking the election of a President Kamala Harris to the democratic traditions and norms of the United States.

As the sticks became unbound by the scarf, so did the United States become unbound from its democratic principles.

The dream had predicted an untethered, disintegrating democracy, fuelled only by its deep divisions. By failing to elect Ms Harris, the nation had allowed the Presidential Candidate with the power to hold everything together, to blow away in the wind.

Writing these passages, I am shocked by how long it has taken me to admit this, even to myself. Despite living in an entirely different country, without any power to vote in the election, my misinterpretation of the dream's symbolism leaves me feeling heavy of heart, almost as though I helped the United States to lose its democracy. Of course, this is nonsensical thinking. Dreams are notoriously complex, highly symbolised, and a person cannot be reasonably expected to perfectly decipher every dream. It has also been difficult to express what I have since come to believe was the true meaning of my dream. Until now. Some things are just easier to say in writing.

Just a case of End Times Fascism?

There is no need to be religious if your end goal is to harness the power of apocalyptic religious narratives. Plenty of powerful leaders around the world, even those who are entirely secular in their beliefs, are building massive empires and political power structures that mirror the sequence of events outlined in Bible prophecy. The question is, are they simply taking advantage of a delusory world, or are they just as unaware as everyone else as to their role in Humanity's foretelling?

The fascist scheme

At the centre of a fascist strategy is a storyline that speaks of a world collapsing under its own weight, leaving just a chosen few to survive and thrive in purpose-built "freedom cities" or underground bunkers. A small group of people, generally of billionaire wealth status, recognise the opportunities that biblical prophecy can bring. The order of the day is to distribute fear among the masses, while simultaneously redesigning the world for self-advantage.

Modern religion allows its most fervent believers to cling to eschatological visions that transcend the "here and now". The result is a world that gives lip service to, or at times even ignores the most vulnerable in need including the world itself, in favour of "eternity in Christ's Kingdom". What lacks in this belief-system is the obvious question of why a deity would want to spend eternity with a group of humans who don't care about anything except their own selfish salvation? And who in their right mind would want to spend eternity with a deity who let humans like that into His Kingdom?

Even more concerning is the cadre of modern power brokers aspiring to transcend Earth's limitations without truly valuing its abundant life. Instead of prioritising the preservation of our planet's rich biodiversity, these elite actors pour their vast fortunes into creating isolated futures. They plan for a world where only a privileged few, supported by cutting-edge technology and massive fortunes, will survive and thrive in artificially constructed enclaves. It is an eery echo of ancient scripture, involving the ones who assume near-divine authority unleashing a deluge upon the rest of Humanity.

It is not just the self-serving among us who have fallen into a fatalistic mindset. A broader revival of apocalyptic thinking has permeated society, and the most vulnerable are the disenchanted masses, who have stopped trusting mainstream messaging, credible thought leaders and traditional news sources and instead are gravitating towards social media influencers and political talking heads.

What used to be research, investigation and evidence-based information reporting is now tabloid journalism and angertainment. Click-bait "news" breeds a form of entertainment focused on building reactionary factions. For many, the promise of societal collapse offers an unexpected emotional refuge. There is a perverse satisfaction found in the anticipation of chaos rather than in the commitment to foster a fair and balanced society.

It is true that the current climate of nihilism, particularly in a nation as powerful and central to the current world order as the United States, is reinforcing a dangerous self-perpetuating cycle of Bible-styled turmoil. This self-reinforcing cycle is predicated on exclusion and domination. It is being deepened every day as political leaders undermine societal safeguards, casting doubt on the efficacy of public protections and collective action. People are being directed towards a survivalist mindset. Meanwhile, an influential class of elite players is seizing each new calamity as an opportunity to privatise essential services and accelerate the gradual dismantling of regulatory frameworks that once protected the public interest.

While the rich prepare their "doomsday" bunkers and encourage the rest of us to "enhance" our consciousness with mobile devices, artificial intelligence tools and subscription services, the average American is slowly becoming repositioned to accept the idea that an impending collapse, like that of End Times Prophecy is near.

Just as stated in Bible prophecy, and the prophecy I encountered, the masses are being trained to distrust the collective and align to a future that is designed to limited ownership, maximise people's reliance on subscription-based services, and replace the human consciousness with an artificial alternative that can be controlled by a select few. Above all else, we are being continuously reminded that we are not enough. We need artificial enhancements of body, mind and spirit, to survive the unavoidable new world. A new world that is being deliberately designed by the very people who are warning us of the danger it brings to Humanity.

It is tempting to believe that those in power have seized opportunities to manufacture apocalyptic events, echoing the prophecies found in the Bible. Over time, mounting evidence suggests that some of these foretold catastrophes have been deliberately engineered for political and strategic purposes.

During the Cold War era, prophecy popularizers turned their focus toward Russia, crafting ominous visions drawn from ancient texts. American televangelist Jack Van Impe, interpreting cryptic passages from the Bible's Ezekiel, warned of a looming "coming war with Russia," shaped by divine foresight. Meanwhile, Jerry Falwell's *Nuclear War and the Second Coming of Jesus Christ* (1983) depicted an all-consuming US-Soviet nuclear conflict, one that would ultimately fulfill the fiery destruction prophesied in 2Peter 3:10 - "The elements shall melt with fervent heat."

In the aftermath of 9/11 and the onset of the Iraq War, prophetic attention shifted from Russia to the Middle East. One key figure in this movement was Lt. General Jerry Boykin, a high-ranking Pentagon intelligence official. Boykin, clad in full military regalia, delivered sermons that cast the war on terrorism in stark, apocalyptic terms before fundamentalist congregations. "Why do radical Muslims hate us so much?" he asked. "Because we're a Christian nation." To Boykin, the battle was more than geopolitical; it was a cosmic struggle against a spiritual enemy "called Satan" whose earthly agents could only be vanquished "if we come against them in the name of Jesus." Even domestic politics, he believed, carried divine significance: "George Bush is in the White House because God put him there for a time such as this."

Paul Boyer, Merle Curti Professor of History at the University of Wisconsin-Madison, recently reflected on a faith-based gathering that took place in January 2025 in Pensacola, Florida. In his article, *Give Me End-Time Religion: The Politicization of Prophetic Belief in*

Contemporary America, published by Yale University, Boyer cited the reaction of an incredulous Canadian journalist: "I have never heard so much venom and dangerous ignorance spouted before an utterly unquestioning, otherwise normal-looking crowd in my life."

The event, led by Tim LaHaye, an influential evangelical Christian minister and author of the best-selling *Left Behind* series, drew approximately 800 attendees, each paying $25 to hear sermons by LaHaye and others. Boyer presented it as a striking example of how powerful entities actively resist international peacekeeping efforts, obstruct conflict resolution, and even anticipate, if not welcome, a coming apocalypse that would lead to the mass extermination of millions.

Further underscoring the mainstream nature of such beliefs, Boyer observed: "Far from being marginalized, these beliefs are pumped into the public arena by high elected officials and pious hucksters, only loosely tethered by denominational or institutional ties, using all the techniques of today's mass media and mass marketing."

The contrary perspective

There are examples of prophetic descriptions discussed in this book that, if artificially engineered to align with contemporary superstitions, would demand an almost impossibly precise manipulation of events.

In a striking example from 2Thessalonians 3-12, Jesus reminds His followers to remain comforted amidst an environment of charlatans who will attempt to distract them from their faith.

*"Let no man deceive you by any means: for that day shall not come, except there come a **falling away** first, and that man of sin be revealed, the son of perdition; Who opposeth and exalteth himself above **all that is called God, or that is worshipped**; so that he as God sitteth in the temple of God, shewing himself that he is God. Remember ye not, that, when I was yet with you, I told you these things? And now ye know what withholdeth that he might be revealed in his time. For the mystery of iniquity doth already work: **only he who now letteth will let, until he be taken out of the way**. And then shall that Wicked be revealed, whom the Lord shall consume with the spirit of his mouth, and shall destroy with the brightness of his coming: Even him, whose coming is after the working of Satan with all power and signs and lying wonders, And with all deceivableness of unrighteousness in them that perish; because they received not the love of the truth, that they might be saved. And for this cause God shall send them **strong delusion**, that they should believe a lie: That they all might be damned who believed not the truth, but had pleasure in unrighteousness."*

These passages reveal several criteria that must be met for End Times events to play out as foretold. Following in an examination of each of the criteria.

A falling away

Before all else, there must be a "falling away" from the true teachings of God. Other parts of the Bible explain this falling away in detail, describing it to be the divergent belief in convenient but false interpretations of God's word, and shifting traditions and idols of worship that gradually decay the original purpose of Christian faith. If considered in isolation, the correct observation would be that this is a phenomenon that has always been present.

For example, in the decades following the New Testament writings, a variety of theological ideas were already circulating among emerging Christian communities. One prominent example was the rise of Gnosticism. Gnostic groups promoted secret knowledge, dualistic views of the world (dividing matter and spirit in stark opposition), and a reinterpretation of salvation that markedly differed from the apostolic teachings.

A few centuries later, debates about the nature of Christ and specifically his divinity animated a large portion of the church. Arianism (318-381 AD), which argued that the Son was a created being and not co-eternal with the Father, created a deep rift.

In the Middle Ages, various groups began to question established practices and doctrines within the institutional church. Although their primary impulse was often to reform and return to a purer form of Christianity, mainstream authorities viewed their challenges as a dangerous departure from traditional faith.

The Enlightenment, along with subsequent scientific advances and the rise of rationalism (18th century) initiated a more widespread cultural and intellectual shift. Over time, especially in Western Europe and North America, this shift led to a broad disaffiliation from traditional Christian beliefs and practices. The trend continued into the 20th and 21st centuries, with religious observance declining markedly, and secular worldviews dominating public life.

The stand-out "falling away" however is the present day. It completely redefines the concept of falling away as being the turn towards an entirely different type of worship. This falling away relates to the worship of political ideology.

The intertwining of faith and politics has led many believers to view political beliefs as central to their spiritual identity. Congregations are increasingly divided as members align their faith with partisan stances, prioritizing political agendas over traditional biblical teachings. This shift is evident in debates over whether pastors should endorse candidates or address social issues from the pulpit. For some, political engagement has become a way to express their faith, while others feel alienated by the growing emphasis on ideology over spiritual unity.

Believers are also turning to politics to navigate complex issues like racial tensions, immigration, and abortion, seeing activism as an extension of their religious convictions. This alignment has reshaped the role of churches, with some embracing political discourse as integral to their mission, going so far as to propagate that one political party is the party of Christ, and the other, the party of "demons". This goes far beyond the concept of dissent or heresy that applies to previous diversionary eras.

So yes, if taken in isolation it might indeed be correct to assume that a falling away has always existed and therefore has always met the prophetic criteria. However, the phenomenon does not exist in isolation, it co-exists with each of the other verses.

All that is called God or that is worshipped

The 3rd Temple is generally considered to be the structure or principle upon which the Antichrist sits whilst opposing and exalting himself above God. However, the phrase "all that is called God or that is worshipped" implies a broader concept than just a single temple, regardless of how significant that temple might be.

Take for example, the 3 co-equal branches of the United States government. The US President is the head of the Executive Branch, often referred to as the 1st branch. The 2nd branch of government is Congress, otherwise referred to as the Legislative Branch. The 3rd branch in which the Supreme Court of the United States is the highest court, is the Judiciary.

A US president who heads the 1st Executive Branch, nulls the 2nd Legislative Branch, and ignores the rulings of the 3rd Judicial Branch, has essentially exalted himself above all that is called God or that is worshipped. If remaining loyal to the concept of the 1st, 2nd and 3rd branches of government, once all three have been defeated, the victor can claim any of the 3 to be the "3rd Temple".

What do we make of a US President who denies Congress its authority to regulate trade and impose tariffs under Article I, Section 8 of the Constitution? Further, what do we make of a US President who, whilst denying Congress, also disregards a unanimous ruling by the US Supreme Court? Both events took place in April 2025, under President Donald Trump. Is this merely a coincidence? Is it a deliberate Fascist manipulation of End Times narratives? Or is it an example of something else? What if it co-exists with each of the other verse criteria? Does it provide a clue about the purpose of prophecy?

He who now letteth will let

According to Biblical prophecy there is a force that is currently holding back evil or lawlessness from taking over. This restraint will continue until the restraint is removed, allowing the Antichrist to fully emerge. This may relate to the "man who will reverse his retirement" phrase in the 1980s prophecy that I encountered. There are alternative interpretations as to who or what the restrainer is. Some theologians believe it to be a Holy Spirit. Others rely on verses such as Romans 13:1-4 which describe governing authorities as instruments of God. Archangel Michael is suggested to be the restrainer, based on his role in spiritual warfare as described in Daniel 10:13 and Revelation 12:7. The Church is also an option, given that some believe its presence and prayers to act as a barrier against the rise of evil.

There is another alternative that is not often given sufficient scholarly credit, and that is the divine spirit that exists within humanity. When the concept of Church or organised religion is removed from the Christian faith, say for example as appears in Gnosticism, humanity is interpreted to be the entity possessing an inherent capacity to reflect a universal power as described in Genesis 1:26-27.

If humanity were to give its power away to something else, perhaps something synthetic like artificial intelligence, would that be the moment in which it foregoes its restraint and allows the full extent of the power of the Antichrist to be unleashed?

What if traditionally powerful institutions, such as large law firms, universities, security agencies, political parties, foreign nations, and other groups, began falling into line with mandates set by the US President? Would this be a sign of this criterion of the verses being fulfilled?

The strong delusion

The Bible states that God allows a percentage of people to perish in the final reckoning by allowing a "strong delusion" in the form of a "lie" to not only distract them from their faith, but to encourage them to revel in the pleasure of "unrighteousness". These people will be identified by their diversion from true faith.

Similar occurrences appear in history. For example, in the period surrounding the Roman siege of Jerusalem (70 AD), the actions of the Roman military leaders fulfilled several of the criteria: the full extent of lawlessness was unleashed, traditional faith was sidetracked by a deceptive promise of secular salvation, and many people came to revel in unrighteousness. By some accounts, the Roman General, Titus, was exalted to such an extent that he demanded to be worshipped like God.

Another example appears in the 2nd century BC, during which Antiochus IV Epiphanes desecrated the temple in Jerusalem, imposed a false cult, and led people away from their traditional devotion. His self-exaltation and promotion of counterfeit salvation resulted in extreme lawlessness and a widespread embrace of unrighteousness.

Collectively, history shows that there have been several times when the criteria for End Times prophecy may have been playing out, at least as it relates to a man of lawlessness, a falling away from true faith, a big lie permitted by God to distinguish between the truly faithful and those who are not, and a revelling of unrighteousness. But the prophecy I encountered in the 1980s adds another layer that makes the events of the current day stand out in striking ways.

The person who meets all the criteria of Antichrist, or who promotes Antichrist energy among the people, or who becomes the catalyst for Antichrist events to take place, must meet all the criteria set by the prophecy I encountered, plus the criteria set by Bible prophecy.

In the first instance, he must have 5 letters in his last name. He must also forge an unholy alliance with another world leader, with 5 letters in his name.

The pool of candidates is indeed very narrow.

In order for fascist forces to deliberately set up a series of events that fit the ever-narrowing criteria of End Time Prophecy, so that the powerful can destroy the current world order and replace it with a new world order, complete with Beast and 3rd Temple and every other 2000 year old religious narrative, the impossible would need to be possible.

It will have needed to be a strategy that was planned from the start, during a time when the Bible was being created. Technological advancement to the degree of synthetic consciousness would need to have been visualised and anticipated, and every billionaire on Earth would need to be in on the game.

Is there an explanation for what is happening?

The quick answer to the question of whether there is an explanation of how End Times narrative could be playing out exactly as written 2000 years ago, in Bible prophecy and supported by the prophecy that I encountered on the coffee table of a friend's home in the 1980s, is YES. There is an explanation, which is that we are living a scripted reality.

Life is unfolding exactly as it was foretold more than 2000 years ago. We need to stop being so logical and rational and intelligent and protective of our professional and personal credibility, that we willingly choose to become blind to what is directly in front of us. However, we also must stop being hyperbolically devout to the apocalyptic lens by which we view events that appear to align with prophecy.

It's time to step back, take a breath, and reconsider what lies before us. If it isn't some ancient, elitist blueprint secretly orchestrated by billionaires (because it isn't), and if it isn't God's decree of inevitable doom (which it most certainly is not), then what is it? More importantly, can we transform it into something meaningful, something constructive?

The present day was foretold thousands of years ago. Let's move forward with this shift in perspective and see if the shift helps us to identify how we can use the power bestowed upon us by our Creator to shape the best future possible, for the Earth and for ourselves.

The link between duality and prophecy

The varying interpretations of duality, as outlined in Chapter Ten, show that regardless of the discipline or doctrine, reality is demonstrated to be comprised of interwoven and interconnected principles. These principles may appear to be separate and in conflict with each other, or singular and standing alone, but there is evidence to suggest that these are misconceptions that may provide a key to controlling our future.

In the scientific exploration of reality, a scientific method combining empirical evidence, observation and experimentation is used to gain understanding of the natural world. The scientific method involves forming hypotheses, conducting experiments, analysing data, and drawing conclusions. Peer review and reproducibility are essential to ensure that findings are credible and consistent. Science does not conclude to have achieved factual results until each of these processes has concluded, and the results are consistently the same.

Peer review and reproducibility relies on the idea that reality will repeat itself in a controlled environment. But what if that is not entirely the case? Is it possible that reality cannot be controlled through scientific means, and that reproducibility is determined by something or someone higher than science?

In direct contrast to science, religion often relies on faith, scripture, and tradition as its foundational pillars. Faith involves belief in the unseen or the divine, often without empirical evidence. Scriptures, such as the Bible, Quran, or Bhagavad Gita, provide teachings, stories, and moral guidelines. Tradition encompasses rituals, practices, and customs passed down through generations, shaping the identity and community of believers.

Additionally, religion often draws upon personal experiences, spiritual revelations, and the collective wisdom of religious leaders and scholars. It serves as a framework for understanding life's mysteries, offering meaning, purpose, and ethical guidance. When it comes to the overall interpretation of reality, religion allows for unknown, unproven things to be possible, but only within the parameters set by existing, often ancient interpretations.

Beyond science and religion is the broader idea of Ufology. Ufology is traditionally the study of unidentified flying objects (UFOs) but is also the most common term used to describe an expanded exploration of extraterrestrial intelligent life. Ufology relies on a mix of anecdotal evidence, eyewitness accounts, photographic and video documentation, radar data, and government reports. While it often lacks the rigorous empirical methods of science, ufologists analyse patterns, investigate sightings, and explore phenomena that challenge conventional explanations. Some also delve into historical records and cultural interpretations of aerial phenomena, blending scientific inquiry with speculative theories about extraterrestrial life or interdimensional entities. In more recent years, Ufology has begun to examine possible links between the interdimensional and the spiritual.

The broadness and increasing receptiveness and flexibility of Ufology makes it a fascinating field that sits at the intersection of science, speculation and faith. It is an example of a style of enquiry that does not limit itself to what is already known or universally accepted. It allows for anything to be possible, which subsequently makes it possible for anything to be observed, acknowledged and understood in its true context.

Ufology is an example of how the concept of "normal" is being challenged and redefined, by the curious among us who do not necessarily rely upon preset parameters of science or religion. Of course, it can subsequently produce a lot of flawed speculation, crazy conspiracy, and just plain nonsense. But it is also the most jealously coveted area of US government research and has proven to be the toughest nut to crack when it comes to government transparency and disclosure. Is this a clue that government Ufologists might be onto something?

Ufology is intriguing because it blends disciplines, drawing from a wide range of ideological styles. The styles include quantum physics, spirituality, cosmology, exobiology, trans dimensionality, metaphysics, conspiracy, psychology, sociology, technology, plus esoteric and occult philosophies. As much as scepticism and ridicule encircle ufology, there is much to be admired in terms of its open-mindedness. Openness to the unknown invites discovery, transforming uncertainty into the gift of newfound understanding.

Re-examining Normal

Taking a leaf from the field of ufology, and particularly its embrace of the unconventional, consider the prophecy's use of the phrase "unholy alliance". The "unholy" labelling is often misinterpreted to mean satanic, against God, or blasphemous. However, when the term is examined with proper consideration given to language interpretation, the unholy alliance of the two men simply means that by normal or ordinary standards, they aren't meant to be joined in alliance. They are meant to be divided or opposed to one another. For example, the Democratic US President and an authoritarian foreign leader would normally be divided or opposed. The alliance is therefore unholy considering an understanding of "normalcy" that would ordinarily prevent such an alliance from ever occurring.

Donald Trump announced the start of his 2016 presidential campaign on June 16, 2015. This moment, marked by his now famous escalator entrance at Trump Tower, set the stage for a presidential campaign that would reshape American politics, along with its understanding of normalcy.

Ten years has now passed. The United States has changed significantly, domestically and as an international entity. All 3 branches of US government have been altered in ways that demonstrate a dramatic shift in the lines of 'normalcy'.

In terms of the Executive Branch, Trump's administration has reshaped the presidency by emphasizing executive orders and direct communication through social media. President Trump's approach to governance has often bypassed traditional norms, leading to significant policy shifts, such as immigration restrictions and trade tariffs.

Trump's presidency has deepened partisan divides in Congress, with Republicans largely aligning with his agenda and Democrats opposing it. The presidential impeachment trials against Mr Trump during his first term in office highlighted these divisions, as the impeachment votes, whether to impeach or acquit, were split almost entirely along party lines.

One of the most significant shifts in US governance has been felt by the Judicial Branch. President Trump's appointment of 3 Supreme Court justices in his first term solidified a conservative majority that has influenced rulings on key issues of Constitution and Democracy like abortion and gun rights. His judicial appointments extended to lower courts as well, leaving a lasting impact on the Judiciary.

The balance of power between the 3 branches of government has shifted in favour of the Executive, which shifts the line of normalcy, away from democracy and towards authoritarianism.

Mr Trump's influence on the United States since he first entered the political arena as Presidential Candidate has often been described as unprecedented, with public figures frequently remarking, "This is not normal." Politicians, journalists, and commentators have used this phrase to highlight actions or rhetoric they perceive as deviating from traditional norms of governance and public discourse.

For instance, during Trump's presidency, his defiance of Supreme Court decisions and controversial policies led some to label his administration as a constitutional crisis. Opinion pieces have criticized the normalization of his behavior, urging political insiders to recognize the gravity of his actions.

Similarly, his influence has extended beyond US borders, shaping political narratives in countries like Australia, where my own domestic leaders have drawn comparisons to his policies. This recurring sentiment underscores the broader debate about Trump's impact on democratic institutions and societal norms.

However, norms are only norms for as long as they are normal. Once the lines have shifted, a new normal begins to emerge. After 10 years of Donald Trump at the forefront of every news cycle, the new normal is not as it was a decade ago. To see an issue in its full light, and to plan or prepare for (or against) its reality, including its strengths, weaknesses, challenges and opportunities, a person must view it in the correct context of its new normalcy.

By continuing to proclaim that a Trump-led United States is "not normal" we are failing to acknowledge the true parameters within which reality exists. Without an accurate perspective, it becomes more difficult to see competing and compatible forces that may be interwoven therein.

The Donald Trump dreams

Dreams can often contain very personal messages, specific to the dreamer. However, I cannot ignore the relevance of my 2 scarf dreams, alongside other dreams that I have had about US political players.

In what context does an ordinary Australian woman with no desire to proclaim herself *psychic* begin to dream about strangers in politics who live and operate tens of thousands of miles away from her home in Australia?

Other than the 2 scarf dreams, there are 2 other stand-out dreams that I consider worthy of discussion in this book.

In mid-April 2020, I had my first ever dream about US politics. At first, I didn't understand the symbolism of the dream, which did not include any political figures specifically. But within a few days I recognised the relevance of the dream. When I did, I recorded the very first video on YouTube that would subsequently lead to me changing my focus, my career and quite frankly my entire perspective on life.

In this dream I saw an ornately carved Maypole. It appeared to be carved from wood, but was entirely painted red. The pole took centre stage of my dream. At its top, several long black strings protruded, each held by stick figured people who were dancing excitedly around the pole, as though they were engaging in a Maypole ritual. I think I recall around 8 or so people were dancing around the pole, which was overly ornamented. It appears the entire point of the pole was to focus everyone's attention upon it. The dancing figures were very lively, noisy and highly distracting, but behind the entire scene I was able to see a solid blue background, like a bricked wall, with nothing other than its colour to define it.

The dream was brief and peculiar, with nothing relevant to my life that I could identify. Within a few days and considering other dreams that had been vaguer and more difficult to describe in detail, I recognised that this dream signified Donald Trump's place in American thought. He was the ornate red pole, standing in the centre of view. Unmissable, and with the constantly eager attention of everyone dancing around him. He represented the call of the Republicans, or of an anti-Democracy, or perhaps even an anti-Americanism. He was the opposite of what appeared solid and blue behind his distraction – the solid blue wall of Democratic politics, or democratic norms, or the United States itself.

When I finally interpreted the dream's meaning I realised its relevance to the prophecy I had been chasing all these years, and recorded my first video on YouTube, to see if might spark useful or informative conversation. It did.

The second of these dreams took place early Saturday morning, 30th May 2020. I dreamt that I was confined to a small, shadowy space with a handful of other people. One of those people was Donald Trump. He was incredibly angry, and was flying around the room, raging and randomly spitting balls of fire. His appearance was continuously alternating between his usual appearance as a man, and then as a devilish type of creature. He was able to perform supernatural tasks, such as the flying and the fireballs, and other actions that seemed nonspecific.

Mr Trump was the only person I recognised in the room with me. The others were generic people, with no specific identities. I remember feeling terrified in the dream, and at one point Mr Trump held me down and tried to choke me and I was making a point of hiding my fear and acting defiant. I recall saying "I'm not afraid of you!", but that was clearly a lie. I was indeed very afraid in the moment, which is an unusual feeling for me while I'm dreaming. I will generally observe the activities of a dream without feeling fear. I do sometimes feel anxiety or sadness if I dream about losing a pet, but I don't recall ever feeling afraid for myself in a dream.

I woke up feeling the need to catch my breath, as though I had stopped breathing for a moment. In the first few seconds after waking, I could still feel Mr Trump's weight on my chest and the pressure of his hands around my throat. I immediately got out of bed and recorded a contemporaneous account of my dream which I shared with my social media audience.

This dream has never left me. I sometimes refer to it as the dream to end all dreams. In some ways it changed me as a person, because I discovered something a few months later that always left me wondering. I discovered that at the precise moment that I was having this dream, President Trump, his wife, his youngest son, and a small handful of Whitehouse aides were being rushed to the Whitehouse bunker by the Secret Service. This occurred in direct response to a riot that had broken out during which rioters had broken through temporary fencing erected around the Whitehouse perimeter.

Conflicting reports exist about this incident. In some news reports, unnamed sources claim that President Trump was furious about being forced to move to the confined space, and that he had flown into a rage once inside the bunker. Other reports quote Mr Trump, saying that he "briefly inspected the bunker" earlier that day "just in case it was needed one day".

Riots and protests had been raging for three days by the time I had my dream, in response to the unlawful killing of George Floyd, by a police officer in Washington, a death that was recorded in its entirety by a young public bystander, on her personal mobile device. The news of the killing and subsequent protests had become nightly news across the world, including Australia.

However, the news of the Whitehouse bunker was not known to me until much later, in October 2020, when I happened to see it briefly mentioned in an unrelated New York Times article online.

When I had this dream, I had only been recording videos for social media for around 4 weeks.

It might seem strange to discuss dreams that I have had in this book. Superficially, it seems as though I am attempting to inject myself into a news story, for attention or profit, in a similar way as has been discussed in Chapter Six. But my purpose for doing so is not to demonstrate anything notable about myself. I am nothing other than a normal, average person. I don't have any supernatural abilities; no more than any other person might have.

I believe that I have had these dreams to evidence something relatively untapped within each of us. We all can see reality, whether during our dreams, or with other types of "knowing". But the mistake we make is either to disregard the knowledge, undermine it, or overinflate it until we've perceived ourselves to possess superpowers that set us above others.

The moment we decide that we are psychic and therefore in possession of a special skill, we are favouring ourselves and our singular identity, over something far more important – the message.

The messages we receive in dreams and during periods of meditation, are pieces of a puzzle. Everyone has a piece or pieces. We should be focusing on putting those pieces together, rather than holding them to ourselves, as though they are proof of our special uniqueness.

It is only strange to write a book filled with historical facts related to war, economics and US presidents, intermingled with prophecies and dream interpretations, because we have decided that it is strange. If we decided that presidential elections, prophecies and dreams, along with extraterrestrial life, karma and any other number of topics are all interwoven into a dualistic reality then it will no longer be strange to consider them collectively.

From Western prophecy to Eastern folklore

The Chinese system of faith, Taoism can be traced back to ancient China, with its roots in prehistoric folk religions and philosophies. Taoism as a formal philosophy is often associated with Laozi (Lao Tzu), traditionally regarded as its founder. His work, the Daodejing (Tao Te Ching), is considered one of the foundational texts of Taoism and is dated between the 8th and 3rd century BCE.

However, elements of Taoist thought existed even earlier, during the Shang dynasty (1600–1046 BC), where practices related to nature, divination, and harmony began to emerge. The Yellow Emperor, Huangdi, who ruled in the 3rd millennium BC, is also linked to Taoist origins, as his teachings influenced later Taoist philosophy

In Taoism, the concept of yin and yang serves as a foundational principle, illustrating the harmonious interplay of opposing forces within the universe. Rather than conflicting or competing, yin (representing qualities like darkness, femininity, and passivity) and yang (symbolizing light, masculinity, and activity) are seen as complementary and interdependent. Their dynamic relationship underpins the natural order, emphasizing balance and the interconnectedness of all things. This interwoven dualism teaches that both forces are essential, as they together create wholeness and enable the cycles and rhythms of life, such as day turning into night, or stillness giving way to movement.

Beyond Taoism, dualistic realities emerge in diverse domains. In religion, many traditions explore the interplay between good and evil, heaven and earth, or the divine and mortal realms, highlighting the necessity of balance in spiritual growth. Extraterrestrial beliefs often frame duality through notions of known versus unknown, terrestrial versus alien life, or science versus mystery. Similarly, science itself operates within dual frameworks—order and chaos, energy and matter, creation and destruction. Psychology delves into the duality of conscious and subconscious minds, as well as rational thought versus emotion, to understand human behaviour. Non-religious spirituality echoes this theme, recognizing the dual forces of personal freedom versus collective responsibility, or inner peace versus external challenges. Together, these examples demonstrate the universal presence of dualistic realities, underscoring how interconnected forces shape existence across all realms of thought.

Expanding on the concept of interconnected dualities, one could hypothesize that religion and extraterrestrial theories may complement each other by addressing humanity's shared quest for understanding the cosmos and our place within it. While religion often provides frameworks for spiritual meaning and divine creation, extraterrestrial beliefs may explore similar questions in the context of life beyond Earth, merging metaphysical wonder with the pursuit of cosmic truths. Similarly, science and spirituality could be seen as mutually enriching forces: science probes the tangible workings of the universe, while spirituality reflects on intangible experiences, like purpose and interconnectedness. Together, they might provide a fuller picture of existence, where empirical evidence meets inner wisdom. These dualities suggest that human inquiry thrives not in opposition but in integration, weaving contrasting forces into a more holistic understanding of reality.

Quantum Transformation

In as much as the concept of dualism infers competing or interdependence, it may also infer a point in the prophetic timeline of events where a decision needs to be made. The decision appears like a point of interference, and the choices act as forks in the road of prophecy. As the decision is made, an immediate recalibration of the prophetic script occurs. In the context of dualism, it may recalibrate as a complementary interdependence, or as conflicting opposites.

Kamala Harris's unexpected, vibrant and short-lived presidential campaign during the 2024 election cycle, might have been an example of such a point of time in the prophetic timeline. Richard Nixon's presidency and its unique resemblance in many ways to what we are currently experiencing in the Trump presidency, may be another. Is there a possibility that interwoven dualistic forces collided during specific points in the timeline that required a choice to be made to calibrate the script and continue forward?

Every transformative journey begins with a spark – a seemingly insignificant moment that quietly shifts our inner landscape, much like a butterfly's delicate wingbeat sets the stage for a powerful ripple. Even the tiniest internal shift can catalyse a monumental leap in our lives and influence society at large. This transformation is not random; it is a deliberate interplay between our inner reality, the tangible world we inhabit, and the profound invitation to embrace a purpose that transcends ordinary existence.

Our inner world is a reservoir of thoughts, feelings, dreams, and unspoken narratives that collectively shape our perceptions and determine our actions. It collects, compounds, and acts like a blueprint, a place where emotions, beliefs and imagination blend seamlessly to construct our unique reality. Everything is energy, and energy is continuously in motion. It is dynamic, often setting the stage for the challenges and triumphs we face externally, whether it be as individuals or as a collective.

In the outer world, our gaze is cast onto a tangible, ever-shifting external landscape. The physical environment, societal structures and cultural dynamics all influence our daily lives. Often, our surroundings act as a mirror, reflecting the energy and mindset that we project from our inner world. Many of us recognise this in our own lives. Chaotic personalities tend to attract chaos into their lives. Kindness towards others will generally result in kindness reciprocity. Like attracts like, and most people have experienced this phenomenon throughout their lives.

However, the like attracts like phenomena is not limited to individual personal interactions. It sits within a wider concept of societies mirroring the temperaments of their deities. This wider theory has been a subject of philosophical and anthropological exploration for centuries.

For example, renowned psychologist, Sigmund Freud suggested that early human societies projected their internal struggles onto divine figures. Freud theorised that gods were shaped as extensions of primal human desires and fears, reflecting the collective psyche of their worshippers. Peaceful deities emerged in societal thought as gods who sought stability, and vengeful gods mirrored tumultuous or authoritarian periods for humanity.

The German philosopher, Friedrich Nietzsche expressed a similar theory about moral systems designed by humanity and projected onto the gods they worshipped. When societies favoured "masters", they worshipped gods who embodied strength, vitality and freedom. When they favoured "slave morality" societies worshipped deities promoting submission, guilt and vengeance.

Whether it be on the micro or macro scale, our environment shapes our experiences, and in return, our internal state can alter the very fabric of the world around us.

Drawing inspiration from the world of physics, the concept of "wave interference" emerges. Wave interference is the observable phenomena in which waves in a medium can amplify each other through "constructive interference" (complementary interdependence). Alternatively, waves can cancel each other out in "destructive interference" (conflicting opposites). Our, internal intentions and external realities co-exist in a similar way. It is dualistic reality playing out every day, all around us.

When our thoughts, feelings and actions align harmoniously, they produce a resonance that propels positive change. Conversely, when there is discord within, the resulting cognitive dissonance can lead to turmoil and miscommunication. A delicate balance is required to create a life of harmony and fulfilment.

At the heart of this is the concept of being "chosen", a term which appears frequently in the Bible and other religious writings, but which I believe has been misinterpreted. In its truest sense, being chosen is a prelude to transformative change. Transformation occurs, when a decision is made by the individual, and by the collective, based on singular and group callings from within. We are each beckoned toward a greater, more meaningful existence in ways that are subtle yet persistently nudging at us, urging us to lead, heal and innovate. To say that only a few thousand people, in a world of 8 billion, are the chosen few, is ridiculous. It presents an impossible task for those claiming to be chosen ones, and for the world at large. But to recognise that we are each chosen, makes perfect sense. We are chosen to search within us for the piece of the puzzle that we can provide, so that collectively we can transform our path every time its dualistic nature presents a wave interference. We choose a harmonious alignment of the waves of reality and move forward into a constructive continuation of the script. Alternatively, we choose a disruptive misalignment of the waves and move into a new path of destructive recalibration.

Either way, we are designing our own reality, by making minor adjustments in everyday life, across multiple simultaneous frameworks, that respond by leading us towards an unforeseen, monumental change in our reality.

There is a severe underestimation and underappreciation of the power of self-awareness, and the even greater power available to each of us, and which plays a role in the evolving tapestry of our collective destiny.

Using the Richard Nixon presidency as an example, the framework of reality that existed during his time in office had a similar type of energy to the presidency of Donald Trump. This was so much the case that certain individuals who felt closely aligned to Nixon, the most notable example being political strategics, Roger Stone, also gravitated towards Trump. They became his fiercest allies, even going so far as to articulate their perception of many similarities between Nixon and Trump. Nixon left office before his intended term was complete. He wasn't forced to leave, but he had been warned that if he didn't, he would be facing criminal indictment. What if he had stayed? Would the United States have transformed itself into a new style of nation long ago? Was the decision to indict Nixon an act of collective consciousness that ultimately held a transformation of the world order at bay? Could this have been the remnant of a past prophetic wave, its interference shaping the choices made and ultimately delaying the unfolding of the script by decades?

In a similar vein, consider the surprise presidential campaign of Kamala Harris. She exploded onto the scene with her announcement that she was intending to run for President on 21 July 2024, only 15 weeks prior to election day. Her campaign immediately took flight, inspiring tens of millions of Americans to attend her rallies, contribute to her campaign, and vote for her.

Given the limited 15-week campaign period, Kamala Harris's popular vote margin of 3.6% reflected a significant challenge in mobilising voters and establishing a robust campaign presence. The margin was clear and underscored the difficulty of competing against Donald Trump, who had been continuously campaigning since mid-2015. Mr Trump had a longer-established base and a consistently solid messaging platform. Harris's atypically short timeframe limited her ability to sway undecided voters and build momentum in key battleground states.

However, a 3.6% margin in the popular vote is extremely impressive for a surprise, time-condensed campaign: or indeed any campaign.

The question is, was the Kamala Harris campaign a clue as to how to bridge inner visions to the realities of physical experience? Rather than wait for the next wave interference, humanity can create one in the image it wants to move forward with. This is something fully understood by Donald Trump, who is demonstrating again and again that his greatest power is that of disruption. Routinely, the world has focused on excitedly reacting to Trump's every move, every statement and every social media post. Just like the nondescript stick figured humans in my Maypole dream.

Since the November 2024 presidential election, I have been urging people to unite with one another. In a nation deeply divided, depressed by the endless news cycle of shadowy doomsday predictions, and alongside the practical disempowerment of the US democratic processes, it seems necessary to choose from what seems to be a brief spectrum of alternatives, On one side of the spectrum, a person could feel entirely defeated, as though there is nothing left to do but wait for the world to end. Perhaps if we are very lucky, an extraterrestrial craft will appear in the sky, filled with supreme alien beings who intervene on humanity's behalf and fix it all. But humanity itself is virtually powerless. The only hope we have is that perhaps we are too old to see it happen in its entirety. This is a frame of mind that has been voiced many times by a variety of people on my social media platform. It is a very real feeling that many people have.

On the other side of the spectrum, an angry population of Resistance Fighters has formed. They attend every protest march, gather online to declare their refusal to accept the election results, plot their next protest, and actively boycott the hundreds, or possibly thousands of companies that are falling into line with the Donald Trump presidency.

The spectrum is also mirrored by an entirely opposite group of people, ranging from illogically elated, to fervently prescribed to the theory that their beloved President is a victim of an elitest world-wide strategy to 'cancel' them.

In the centre of it all lies the silent majority. The ones who watch all sides and spectrums from somewhere in the middle. These are the people who may agree with some principles from the Left, and some from the Right. But mostly they just want to live and be happy. They want to surround themselves with people, pets and experiences that they love, create a life that they can look back on with pride, and to maintain a life of peace, with hobbies, fresh air, and abundance.

To all readers, regardless of where you sit on the various spectrums, preoccupations and beliefs. I ask that you imagine, for a moment, a quantum leap of sorts. A leap so profound that it transforms individual lives and ignites a widespread ripple effect across society. And then, across multiple societies. The term "quantum" relates to the smallest of things, and a quantum transformation is one in which a merge of the personal with the collective occurs with the implementation of tiny yet persistent changes. The smallest of shifts can have vast implications that ultimately lead to human evolution.

In some ways, quantum physics (the scientific study of the smallest things that exist), and spiritual awakening are the same thing. They begin with a tiny change, barely perceptible to the naked eye, highly "contagious", and readily accessible to every person on Earth. The change begins to grow, first slowly, hardly a ripple effect to be seen. But with persistence it continues, until the ripples become waves, and waves tsunamis. Not a single tsunami as is often dreamt of in politics, in which one side violently washes out the other. But a series of cumulative tsunamis that create wave interference against the status quo.

One of the most inspiring quotes I've ever known comes from an unexpected source. Buckminster Fuller was a futuristic architect, born in Milton Massachusetts in 1895. He died in 1983 after having brought a variety of innovative structures to life with his architectural designs. Just prior to his passing, he was interviewed by Mike Vance and Diane Deacon, co-founders of the Creative Thinking Association of America. The interview was non-remarkable and was part of a wider concept of gaining insight from a variety of creative thinkers.

During the interview, which took place in an ordinary motel room in Santa Monica, California, Mr Fuller made a brief statement that was later immortalised in a book co-authored by Vance and Deacon called *Think Outside the Box (1995)*. He said:

> *"You never change things by fighting the existing reality.*
> *To change something, build a new model that makes the existing model obsolete."*

We have a habit of separating ourselves into two distinct groups of people. In one group sits a small percentage of the world population: politicians, powerbrokers, famous voices, celebrities, influencers, notorious personalities, sports heroes, and long-ago deceased people of wisdom and insight. These people stand out to us, we know their names, they say inspirational, entertaining or radical things, and in practical terms they are outside of our reach.

The rest of us, the humongous majority, sit in the other group. We are conscious of the first group to varying degrees and spend our time waiting for someone from that group to do something that will make a practical positive difference to the second group. Alternatively, we may be treading water in our day-to-day existence or working hard to find an entrance path into the first group.

This habit that we have, is never going to create a new model that makes the existing model obsolete. Never. It will only ever allow some people from the first group to slide occasionally down to the second group, and some from the second group to elevate themselves to the first group. But reality will never change.

The reason why this model will never change is because our sense of "normal" relies upon the idea that only some of us are "chosen". The concept of being one of the "chosen few" may or may not have been contrived to keep humanity trapped inside a prison of self-doubt. Certainly, within Gnostic thought, it is believed that dark forces, and earthly agents of those dark forces, are engaged in controlling humanity through reinforced patterns of fear, division and self-disempowerment. According to the Gnostics, religion is one of the methods by which people are suppressed. They are redirected away from their own sense of empowerment (referred to as "the inner light"), and towards the preoccupation with traditions, rituals, normalcy and an unreachable, all-powerful divinity that resides far away in an outer realm.

Gnosticism, Kabbalah, Taoism, Hinduism, Buddhism, and even the "fringe" beliefs held by Raëlianism, a UFO-based religious movement founded in 1974 by Claude Vorilhon (Raël), carry a range of interpretations that somehow converge into a single radical view that each of us is chosen. We are each the "God" that we have been trained to believe lives outside of us.

If this is true, and if we possess the "God" element within, then we also have the individual and collective power to transform our reality. Each of us is a piece in the puzzle of what use to be, what exists now, and what can be ours in the future. We each have a quantum spark of empowerment, and we each are chosen.

The way forward

This is not the first book to discuss personal and collective empowerment, the light of an inner divinity residing in each person on Earth, or the transformative influence of collective action. These concepts have been examined for hundreds, thousands of years.

To correctly place these thoughts into the context of the prophecy examined in this book, and to weave together the intricate threads that comprise the prophecy and its implications, we need to return to the source of everything that is and ever was - God.

God's place in Prophecy

God is where it all begins. In the Bible, and all preceding religious doctrine, along with all that is foretold through biblical prophecy, God is the divine aspect that links it all together. So, who or what is God?

To understand God is to first understand where the term "God" originally derives. It did not come from the Bible. It also did not come from any other religious or faith-based writings. The word "God" has its roots in the Proto-Germanic word *gudan* which derives from an earlier Proto-Indo-European word *ghut* or *gheu* meaning "to invoke". The earlier language structure arose from the Late Neolithic to Early Bronze Age (4500-2500 BC).

The term originated during a time of significant cultural and technological developments, including the domestication of animals, the advent of agriculture, and the use the metal tools. The Proto-Germanic speakers were evolved migrants of the earlier group who resided in the geographic proximity of what is now Ukraine and Russia (500 BC to 500 AD).

The worldview of these people was largely influenced by their pastoral lifestyle, which emphasised mobility, kinship, and a connection to nature. They lived within a patriarchal social structure and had a polytheistic faith system that was centred around natural forces and superstitions and protective rituals. The Proto-Germanic language overall, was closely related to lifestyle elements, such as agriculture, animal husbandry, and social hierarchy.

In a practical way, the early word *ghut/gheu* was tied to daily rituals. The word was an expression of invocation, and so it was a way to bring attention to something in the environment that must transform, grow, or yield reward. Early spiritual practices were deeply connected to survival and prosperity. A person will have used the word as an expression of acknowledgement of their own role in creation of a successful harvest, or to express gratitude, or seek favourable outcomes. The term was tied to blessings bestowed upon crops, livestock, and other aspects of life. The term then evolved into one related to rituals and other invocations, and expanded to include acknowledgement of external influences, such as deities or unknown positive forces.

The term evolved into "God", during the development of the Old English language structure (500-1100 AD approx.). By this time the word was referring to a deity or supreme being. In its originating state, the term was tied to acts of worship or invocation but later began to possess ethical or moral connotations more closely resembling today's contextual understanding.

The word "God" was used in the English translations of the Bible as a replacement word for the many names that refer to an entity or entities of supreme power in the original compilation of the Hebrew Bible (*the Tanakh*), consisting of 24 books, which have generally been rearranged into what is now the Old Testament.

The names originally appearing in the Hebrew Bible include Elohim, Yahweh, Adonai, El Shaddai, and Elyon, along with other inferred descriptors, all of which have been replaced with the word "God". In some cases, this has meant that during the story unfolding, God may appear to be called "Lord God", or "God God".

For example, in Genesis 2:4-5 the original Hebrew Bible refers to "Yahweh Elohim" on 2 occasions. Yahweh is a name and Elohim is a word relating to multiples, a group or family. The correct translation in English would identify that Yahweh comes from a group of entities, like how a person today may say "John from the Smith Family". However, because the word "God" is used twice, it is translated to say "God God". In some interpretations this is changed to "Lord God". Either way, the translation demonstrates that the original intention for the Hebrew wording has been misinterpreted. This is an anomaly that occurs when languages evolve and words start to take on new meanings. In a 2000-year-old text, the interpretative flaws become evident.

There is a real possibility that the word God is a diversion from what is more precisely an inner power to invoke transformation. The original Hebrew words of the Bible may in fact be speaking of something entirely different. There are a growing number of researchers and theologians who claim that the original Hebrew Bible is not a book about God, it is a book about some other type of being, whether that means a different incarnation of ourselves, or even extraterrestrial or interdimensional beings. Those ideas sit outside the parameters of this book. However, they do demonstrate that originally, we believed ourselves able to invoke transformation. It was only through the process of evolution, that we gave that job to God.

What is the Purpose of Prophecy?

The traditional view of prophecy is that it serves several purposes. Firstly, it reminds us that God has devised a grand plan that He intends to unfold. Nothing happens by chance, and everything around us is part of a broader, divinely orchestrated framework. This is a problem because it means that the awful, cruel and devastating things that happen in the world are unavoidable. They are simply part of a bigger plan.

Secondly, prophecies are at their very core, calls for humanity to repent and live righteously. This presents another problem in that the first reasoning immediately makes this second reason illogical. Why bother repenting or living righteously when those aspects of self ultimately make no difference to God's grand plan?

Prophecy is also explained to be a function of encouragement for the faithful. Through the foretelling of prophecy, the faithful can rest assured that God is always present, always connected to His faithful, and they are never alone. This assurance is meant to provide comfort during times of uncertainty or distress, as it reflects the promise that God remains in control and will ultimately bring about restoration and justice.

When we put these purposes together, they collectively state that God is an arsonist fire-fighter. He deliberately sets fires, some of them thousands of years in advance, so that he can put them out and play Hero. He has left us completely defenceless. We have no power other than to thank him for setting fires and then putting them out. This is not a reassuring message for anyone to hear. If this is the purpose of prophecy, then many people have died or suffered in the fires deliberately set by God. They have been placed into a situation that allows them no ability to escape. Some of those people have been newborn babies, who haven't lived long enough to be faithful believers in God. They are perfectly innocent and completely defenceless. And yet, they are punished, sometimes tortured, simply because God wants to set a fire and then be seen to extinguish it, eventually.

The overall explanation of prophecy in traditional religious thought, is that it validates the idea of an external divine authority. And so, the next question is – what is the purpose of that?

Could it be that the purpose of validating an external divine authority is to distort or camouflage an understanding of the **internal** divine authority?

If indeed, the divine authority over transformational reality is internal, then is it possible that the **true** purpose of prophecy is to give Humanity the ability to see where it can invoke its own divinity? Furthermore, is our divinity the quantum spark from within that allows us to individually and collectively transform our reality?

The John Kerry clue

The 1980s prophecy foretold a transformative juncture marked by the arrival of a US president identifiable by a specific trait: a 5-letter surname. In the fifty years preceding the new millennium, only a handful of potential candidates, notably Richard Nixon and Spiro Agnew, fit this requirement.

After the turn of the millennium, however, the number of potential candidates bearing 5-letter surnames began to rise dramatically. Every presidential cycle since then has featured one or more credible figures who met the criterion. John Kerry was the first in 2004. His surname perfectly fits the requirement, appeared to be in a strong position to fulfill the prophecy. Yet his loss, set against one of the most contentious and closely fought electoral battles in modern history, suggests that prophetic messages may not always align neatly with literal expectations.

Rather than serving as a rigid formula for predicting outcomes, prophecies may operate on more subtle, sequential levels. It is plausible that earlier components of the prophetic narrative are meant to set the stage for later developments. This process mirrors the principles of wave interference. Just as overlapping waves can create patterns of both constructive (interdependent) and destructive (competing) interference, critical moments of disruption in history can amplify or negate forces that, on the surface, seem predictable.

The Bush v. Kerry election embodies this turbulent interplay. Defined by razor-thin margins, protracted legal battles, recounts in Florida, and widespread allegations of voter irregularities, this election cycle was fraught with ambiguity. Had Kerry captured Ohio's crucial 20 electoral votes, he would have met the numerical threshold for victory. It begs the question of whether this near miss was a powerful clue. The John Kerry scenario hints that prophecies might signal key moments of interference and opportunity rather than straightforward outcomes, compelling us to scrutinize the hidden dynamics within the socio-political fabric.

Was the Bush-Kerry race an invitation to observe emerging patterns akin to wave interference? Do these historical moments, when examined closely, reveal subtle signposts that urge us to remain ever vigilant, suggesting that our very observation and interpretation of events might alter their trajectory in much the same way as measurements affect quantum systems? This possibility invites a deeper reflection on how prophecy interweaves with both numerical patterns and the unpredictable forces of change.

The 1939 Pact clue

History offers a sobering lesson: alliances born of expedience rather than shared conviction are prone to betrayal. The 1939 Nazi-Soviet Pact, initially hailed as a pragmatic non-aggression treaty, ultimately became a prelude to one of history's gravest betrayals. Hitler's unexpected attack on the Soviet Union serves as a warning that even meticulously negotiated accords can mask hidden ambitions and unforeseen treachery.

In the modern arena, the reported unholy alliance between Donald Trump and Vladimir Putin draws unsettling parallels to that historic pact. This modern rapprochement, characterized by political opportunism and conflicting strategic interests, hints at a relationship built more on convenience than on genuine trust. Critics observe that such an alliance, much like its historical predecessor, might crumble beneath the weight of its own contradictions, exposing vulnerabilities on a national scale. Whilst an unholy alliance may ordinarily refer to an opportunistic partnership between rivals, the prophecy's subsequent prediction of an attack by Russia indicates that there may be a warning associated with the alliance.

Adding a further twist to the narrative, Viktor Orbán emerges as an alternative figure whose alignment with Trump represents a possible either/or scenario in contemporary geopolitics. Orbán's leadership, noted for its authoritarian tendencies and pragmatic realpolitik, offers a different model of alliance-building.

Whether the future sees the United States embroiled in a Trump-Putin dynamic or an alternative Trump-Orbán coalition, the inherent lesson remains the same. When alliances are forged to serve short-term strategic gains rather than deeply held values, they risk ultimately betraying those very interests. This warning resonates strongly with the prophecy that foretells a weakened US, vulnerable to attacks on its own soil by Russia and other adversaries. The historical betrayal by Hitler in the Nazi pact reminds us that when leaders prioritize transient political expediencies over national integrity, the long-term consequences can be dire. Just as the Nazi pact's collapse precipitated global conflict, a modern-day betrayal, whether from a Trump-Putin alignment or a Trump-Orbán alternative, could weaken the nation's strategic position and sow seeds of division.

Consequently, the enduring message of this prophecy is clear: be ever vigilant about alliances that may appear beneficial in the moment, but which carry the potential for profound betrayal. History implores us not to mistake the appearance of unity for lasting commitment. Instead, close scrutiny is required when dealing with any coalition, whether it be with Putin, Orbán, or another opportunistic partner. If prophecy is intended to highlight points of observable disruption to trajectories, it may also reveal ghosts of past treacheries that are likely to reemerge to devastate the future.

Another Unholy Alliance clue

Throughout history, certain leaders have embodied profound contradictions, captivating segments of the populace while simultaneously inciting equally passionate revulsion. This phenomenon has been particularly pronounced in recent years. Such an enigmatic figure appears to be the living embodiment of an unholy alliance in the literary sense. A convergence where dark and light, attraction and repulsion, intertwine. His magnetic appeal draws admirers who see him as a symbol of change or defiance, while his detractors view him as an agent of chaos. This duality reflects a motif often explored in literature and art, where unholy alliances are depicted as dangerous mergers of opposing forces that both illuminate and corrupt.

The defining characteristics of an unholy alliance within an individual represent a complex interplay between harmful and redeeming qualities, where the light of charismatic allure is inseparable from the shadow of underlying malice. This produces a distinct tension that conceals a deeper truth: power has the capacity to simultaneously inspire adoration and hatred. The man who embodies this archetype today is Donald Trump. He evokes classical imagery of a leader whose qualities mirror the unsettling duality found in both creative expression and the moral dilemmas of human history.

Some commentators extend this analysis to biblical prophecy, drawing potential parallels between Mr Trump and the Antichrist - a figure foretold in scripture to be both charismatic and deceptive, exuding charm while carrying an undercurrent of ruin. Just as the Antichrist is described as a master of seduction, effortlessly forging alliances that challenge traditional moral boundaries, Trump appears to galvanize disparate, often contradictory, factions within society. His public persona, marked by intense loyalty from certain groups and fierce opposition from others, reflects the ancient archetype of the Antichrist - a symbol of ultimate duality and conflicting allegiances that can signal turbulent times.

Ultimately, this embodiment of an unholy alliance challenges conventional perceptions of leadership and morality. The interplay between admiration and animosity, light and dark, suggests that his influence is not solely the product of policy or rhetoric but rather a deeper, more enigmatic synthesis of charismatic magnetism and inherent contradiction. Whether viewed through the lens of literature, art, or biblical prophecy, the lessons remain clear: when a leader encapsulates such duality, he becomes a living metaphor for the turbulent forces that shape societies, urging us to remain vigilant to both the promises and perils embedded within the shadows of power.

I do not believe that Donald Trump is "the Antichrist" creature foretold in prophecy. Rather, I suspect there have been several men throughout history who either embodied Antichrist-like qualities or represented prophetic timestamps linked to the Antichrist archetype. However, an examination of biblical criteria associated with this figure reveals traits that closely align with observable characteristics displayed by Trump. I do believe he has a role to fulfil within the prophetic context, pertaining to exaggeration of past clues. The intention is to encourage us to reexamine pivotal disruption points within the prophetic timeline - moments where we can still recognize and activate choices that remain within our grasp.

Donald Trump appears to align with every prophetic criterion I have been able to observe. To my knowledge, no other individual since the turn of the millennium has met these criteria in their entirety. This, in my view, makes him a significant clue in understanding the deeper intention and purpose behind prophecy.

However, he is not solely responsible for the unfolding events as foretold. If he were, the prophecy would be uniquely personal to him. Instead, my evolving understanding of prophecy suggests that it serves a broader function. It invites collective interception and engagement rather than passive acceptance. Prophecy, rather than being a fixed declaration of fate, may instead act as a mechanism prompting society to recognize pivotal moments and respond accordingly.

In this context, Mr Trump appears to function as a **signal** - a focal point within a larger, dynamic framework. His presence marks interference points that, much like wave interference in physics, disrupt patterns and introduce observable anomalies. These points may serve as indicators that can be identified using modern analytical tools, offering insight into the trajectory of events and the choices available for intervention. Through this lens, prophecy does not simply foretell. It presents a sequence of moments that demand recognition, interpretation, and potential redirection.

A simple illustrative example might be that which occurred during the Nixon Presidency. Were the criteria matches relating to Nixon also signals? Where there points of inference during the Nixon presidency that acted as a prequel for events to unfold in the next millennium? If so, what types of interference points could have been used to shape the trajectory of events related to Nixon? Can a similar disruption and realignment technique be used during interference points yet to come?

The Middle Eastern War clue

If peace in the Middle East were easily attainable, history suggests it would have been achieved long ago. Yet, the region remains embroiled in cycles of violence and upheaval, with even periods of relative calm overshadowed by deeply rooted complexities and competing interests. No era appears to have been completely free from conflict, reinforcing the difficulty of resolving long-standing tensions.

The prophecy I encountered in the 1980s foretold that a cataclysmic world event would be "ignited" by conflict in the Mediterranean region of the East. While I am not able to propose solutions to what has long seemed an unsolvable issue, I have come to wonder whether the specific wording of the prophecy contains a clue. The choice of the word "ignite" suggests something combustible. Something fuelled. Could this prophecy be pointing toward an energy resource, such as oil or gas?

Crude oil has long been considered the most valuable commodity in the Middle East, shaping its economic and geopolitical landscape. The vast reserves underpin the financial stability of nations such as Saudi Arabia, the United Arab Emirates, Kuwait, and Qatar, making petroleum the foundation upon which regional economies and political power are built. Despite efforts to transition away from fossil fuels, oil remains the dominant force in global energy markets, with the Middle East supplying roughly one-third of the world's crude oil. As oil prices continue to influence global energy policies, this resource remains not just a commodity but a geopolitical asset. It has dictated alliances, conflicts, and economic dependencies for generations.

However, recent conflicts in Gaza have shifted attention to another fuel source: natural gas. Some analysts suggest that the strategic interest in Gaza, particularly from world leaders such as President Trump and Israeli Prime Minister Netanyahu, is less about religious or ideological stakes and more about its vast offshore gas reserves. Gaza sits at the heart of emerging energy discussions, positioned as a potential key player in reshaping regional energy markets. More significantly, these reserves offer an opportunity to reduce Europe's dependence on Russian gas, which has been a major factor in recent geopolitical manoeuvring.

If the prophecy's use of "ignite" is indeed tied to fuel resources, then Gaza's gas deposits could play an integral role in a broader, unfolding scenario. The intersection of conflict, energy, and global power shifts suggests that the control and exploitation of resources may serve as a hidden catalyst, one that aligns with historical patterns of energy-driven wars and market disruptions. In this context, the prophecy may not simply act as a warning of regional instability. It might provide a signalling clue about a moment in which energy competition, rather than ideological strife, becomes the defining factor in a conflict involving consequences that extend far beyond the Middle East.

It is the reference to the "downfall of Europe" appearing later in the prophecy that gains my attention. Despite many prophecies predicting a European downfall since medieval times, is it possible that this prophecy demonstrates an actual link between Europe and Middle Eastern tensions?

Could securing alternative fuel sources in Europe, or adjusting global energy dependencies related to Europe, serve as a means of altering the trajectory of conflicts in the Middle East? If energy markets truly hold the key to these unfolding events, then the future may rest not in resolving diplomatic disputes alone, but in confronting the underlying economic forces that sustain them.

The Civil War in Syria clue

Despite the unusual longevity of Syria's civil war, which has been raging for over a decade, it has largely been ignored by mainstream Western reporting.

The Civil War began in March 2011 as part of the "Arab Spring protests". Initially, Syrians demanded democratic reforms and an end to government corruption under President Bashar al-Assad. However, Assad's violent crackdown on protesters escalated tensions, leading to an armed rebellion. Other factors, such as economic struggles, sectarian divisions, and foreign interventions, further fuelled the conflict, turning it into a prolonged war.

Bashar al-Assad, often referred to simply as Assad, was removed from power in December 2024, marking the end of his decades-long rule. His whereabouts remain uncertain, but reports suggest he fled Syria following the collapse of his government. Some sources indicate he may have sought refuge in Moscow, Russia, though there has been no official confirmation. There were also unverified claims that his flight vanished after leaving Damascus, raising speculation about his fate.

Other than the prophetic inference of an ignited series of events originating in or around the Syrian region, other aspects of this war maintain my interest.

In the first instance, the Assad family name was originally al-Wahsh, meaning "the savage". In 1927, Ali ibn Sulayman al-Assad (Bashar al-Assad's grandfather) changed the family name to al-Assad, meaning "the lion". The purpose was likely to enhance social standing and perceptions of political strength. However, al-Assad is the way the Assad family is formally addressed. When Bashar al-Assad is generally referred to, particularly in casual settings, the "al" is dropped, leaving the 5-letters of "**Assad**" to remain as his last name.

The Assad family ruled Syria from 1971, enjoying 3 consecutive generations of leadership. Bashar al-Assad took over from his father in 2000, just prior to the commencement of the prophecy's timeline of events. Every new US President to take office during his period of rule also had 5-lettered last names.

It is a strange series of anomalies in which some of the most notable geopolitical leaders, aligned to other leaders, who align to prophetic descriptions, each have the 5-lettered name requirement.

Is this another clue? Was Assad an example of a constructive point of interference? Is the Syrian civil war a matter to resolve to prevent prophetic outcomes? Is the West's general disinterest in the domestic struggles within Syria an undermining of its relevance to Western democratic survival?

The Reversal clue

As explored in Chapter Six, every US presidency since the turn of the millennium has featured a prominent leader emerging from retirement in an effort to guide others through a period of crisis. Yet, despite their intentions, each of these men ultimately failed in their quest.

There are multiple ways to interpret the circumstances that contributed to their failures. My purpose for writing this book, however, is to examine interpretations that may explain the purpose of prophecy, and specifically the prophecy I saw in the 1980s. My interest is in knowing why the prophecy appears to be coming true, and why is it written as it is.

One perspective that I believe might help in this quest, suggests that these individuals ultimately failed because they lacked sufficient support in their efforts. Instead, they were held to impossible standards, expected to be perfect men delivering perfect outcomes. Could this absence of unwavering backing be the reason why none of them remained in their role long enough to meaningfully alter the trajectory of events?

At the beginning of this book, I mentioned my close affinity with the Rider-Waite tarot deck. One card consistently recalls a question I have been contemplating since rumours of President Joe Biden's age and cognitive decline began circulating in news reports and political discussions: the Three of Cups.

The imagery of the Three of Cups depicts three women dancing in a circle, raising golden chalices in celebration. They rejoice in their successful harvest - achieved through mutual support despite their differences. The overarching message of the card is clear: a collective is only as strong as its weakest link, making it crucial to uplift and support those who bear the weight of leadership or responsibility.

Applying this symbolism to President Biden, does the prophecy offer insight into his decision to reverse his retirement? Biden has repeatedly stated that his return to public service was motivated by a desire to guide the American people through a crisis. Was the pivotal moment the one in which his own political party began to turn against him? If he had received unwavering support, just as he sought to offer support to others, could that have created enough disruption to shift the course of events, altering the trajectory of the 2024 election despite widespread claims that his victory was impossible?

In the wake of the 2024 presidential election, I suspect many people have quietly wondered whether President Biden might have secured a second term had he been afforded the steady support of his own party.

Polls consistently reflected doubts about his physical stamina and concerns over his cognitive ability. However, the media forums reporting these poll results also continuously reinforced the idea that Biden's perceived vulnerabilities were serious "cause for concern." This, in turn, became a powerful influence over public perceptions of his ability to win and lead the country. This would naturally impact public polling accordingly.

The impact of collective perception and its ability to shape reality raises deeper questions about the role of expectation in influencing outcomes. What might have happened if the public had been presented with a consistent message of support for President Biden - if faith in his ability to win the election and lead the nation had been unwavering?

The US President appoints a cabinet of officials, each overseeing a specific department within the federal government, such as Defense, State, Treasury, and Education. These cabinet members must be confirmed by the Senate. They each manage their respective agencies, implement policies, and provide expert advice to the President on critical matters. Their role ensures that governance is not solely dependent on the President's decision-making, allowing the administration to function efficiently through delegation and collaboration.

A strong cabinet is essential to a well-functioning government, as these officials are responsible for shaping policies, responding to crises, and guiding national initiatives. The President serves as the public face of the administration, acting as a diplomat, envoy, and figurehead. But the success of their leadership often hinges on the competence and effectiveness of the cabinet. A capable group of advisors and administrators strengthens the government's ability to govern, negotiate, and lead the country through complex challenges. Additionally, Congress and the Judiciary serve as vital checks and balances to the President's authority, ensuring that no single leader holds unchecked power.

Even in a worst-case scenario, Joe Biden's capabilities were hardly likely to have such a destructive effect on the safety, security and integrity of the United States as was propagated by *allied* lawmakers and public influencers who abandoned or collaborated against him! Perhaps, if Biden had been an authoritarian-styled leader who disregarded the advice of his Cabinet, nullified the power of Congress, and defied Supreme Cour rulings – but he was not. Biden was a staunchly democratic-styled leader, who was careful to seek varied counsel from the advisors around him. There was no actual danger of Biden's cognitive or physical abilities posing a threat to the United States. Nonetheless, he was betrayed by his own party, and in spectacular fashion.

Immediately before referencing Biden's reversed retirement, the prophecy also speaks of those who "will arrive with the idea of supporting themselves." Earlier in this book, I examined the phenomenon in which opportunistic individuals exploit crises for personal gain. However, this phrase can also apply to circumstances that undermine someone who steps out of retirement to support others.

Once again, President Biden's experience provides a clear example. As an avid consumer of US news during this time, I personally witnessed several pro-Biden political pundits, lawmakers, television presenters, and social media influencers suddenly appear on cable news and opinion shows, raising concerns about his capability to lead the country. For a period, they strongly opposed his candidacy, despite identifying as staunch Democrats. Many had previously minimized the Democratic Party's shortcomings while amplifying any perceived failures of the Republican Party.

Yet, on this issue, it was as though they could "smell blood in the water" and sought to protect themselves, even if it meant the Democratic Party suffered in the process. This phenomenon spread across all forms of media and arguably made it impossible for Biden to continue, regardless of whether he was fit to lead. Ultimately, it left his replacement candidate, Kamala Harris, also at a disadvantage, forcing her into the campaign with only 15 weeks to secure victory.

I am among those who continue to wonder whether, under different circumstances, the outcome of the 2024 presidential election could have been rewritten had the signals from prophecy been recognized. I wonder, as many undoubtedly do, whether Biden might have won - regardless of the polls - if the people had defied the prophecy's words and chosen to support him rather than themselves.

This is not to be mistaken for chasing the wind - blindly backing a candidate doomed to defeat. Rather, it speaks to the concept of human divinity and the ability to channel momentum toward something greater than mere opposition.

I raise these questions not to focus solely on Biden's campaign but to illuminate what might be the hidden purpose of prophetic messaging. Is the true intention to highlight the flaws in human responses that continually propel us toward inevitable calamity? Can humanity harness this knowledge and thereby redesign our future?

David Petraeus clue

Rather than leave Joe Biden's example to carry the load of this clue in isolation, another retirement reversal is examined to illustrate the repetitive nature of the prophecy's predictions.

In early 2025, President Trump's appointed Secretary of Defense, Pete Hegseth, became embroiled in a scandal that parallels that of CIA Director appointed by President Obama, David Petraeus. Hegseth was discovered to have been using Signal, an encrypted messaging app, to discuss classified US war plans. The breach raised concerns about the security of sensitive communications and the potential exposure of military strategies when a reporter was mistakenly added to the Signal chat group. Despite widespread criticism (by Democrats), Hegseth remained in his position, with supporters arguing that his track record and effectiveness outweighed the controversy surrounding his communication practices. He was supported by his political allies. This is not to infer that he will always be supported. Hegseth may have already departed his role as Defense Secretary by the time this book is published. However, the Signal app event flags a notable contrast to how David Petraeus was treated by his political allies in similar circumstances.

The David Petraeus scandal involved the revelation of his extramarital affair with biographer Paula Broadwell, which led to security lapses due to the sharing of sensitive information through unsecured channels. The fallout from Petraeus's actions resulted in his resignation as CIA director, marking a swift and definitive end to his tenure in government service. Some Democratic officials and media commentators argued that his resignation was necessary due to the national security risks posed by the affair.

The differing outcomes of these scandals highlight an evolving perception of leadership and accountability. Petraeus's resignation in 2012 reflected a rigid, unforgiving stance on personal indiscretions within positions of power. By 2025, however, the response to Hegseth's actions suggested a shift toward a more pragmatic approach, one that acknowledges flaws but prioritizes other factors over personal missteps. The other factors may include effectiveness and prior accomplishments, or it may be purely political. The factors are not the point; the prioritisation is the point.

This change underscores the power of allowing individuals to be imperfect yet still contribute meaningfully. In Hegseth's case, the argument was that his ability to fulfill his role outweighed his lapses in judgment. Arguably, David Petraeus had a far stronger argument than Hegseth in this regard. The contrast between these two scandals reflects an evolving balance between ethical considerations and the necessity of functional leadership in high-stakes environments.

The Kamala Harris clue

If this book had been written by someone who believed herself to be psychic, the explanations of the dreams within it could easily be dismissed as mere predictions of the future. Alternatively, they might have been seen as the fortunate guesses of an opportunistic individual - one who leveraged her social media presence to attract attention and exploit vulnerable people during a time of societal uncertainty.

However, this book was written by someone who has consistently rejected the label of "psychic." I am not psychic. I'm not, I'm not, I'm not. I am simply an ordinary person who, quite unexpectedly, began experiencing peculiar dreams - dreams completely unrelated to my daily life yet undeniably linked to a prophecy I had been pursuing for decades. I sought to understand why these dreams were happening and how they seemed to correspond with news unfolding overseas.

Though I have long had a personal interest in spiritual matters and divination tools - particularly tarot cards - this never translated into a belief that I possessed the ability to predict the future. In fact, I have always believed that dreams, divination, extraterrestrial phenomena, unexplained sightings, ghosts, fairies, and anything else outside traditional religion, science, or psychology are simply alternate representations of reality. The only distinction is that they lack official recognition within those established fields. I am perpetually undecided about what I believe, but I have a growing sense that scientific theory and intuitive perception are more closely aligned than they often appear to be.

I began taking my dreams seriously when they started directly connecting to global events - events that had no obvious impact on me in Australia. Among them, the most striking were my dreams about Kamala Harris and the scarf.

After examining everything explored in this book, I now believe that the scarf dreams were a key to understanding prophecy itself. Amid the 2020 presidential election season, I - a woman in Australia - dreamt of an American flag-patterned scarf, one that fit only Kamala Harris. Days later, Harris was chosen as the Democratic Party's vice-presidential candidate. The party went on to win the election. Biden and Harris were elected to office.

Had I understood reality back then as part of a larger, interconnected whole, where individuals and collectives shape the world around us, then my decades-long pursuit of a 1980s prophecy and my dream about Harris and the scarf might have been logically connected in my mind. I might have recognized that the dream (one aspect of reality) was revealing that Harris was the only person suited for a particular task in the future. That is why the scarf fit only her. Such an awareness might have led to an understanding of what was to come, fostering a deeper ability to tap into an inner divinity - one that could connect to other forces near and far, perhaps even beyond our world.

I am not suggesting that there was anything I could have done as an individual. But what if, collectively, humanity embraced a broader perception of reality? Peculiar dreams, inexplicable premonitions, angel numbers, déjà vu moments, unexplainable emotions, and fleeting thoughts that seem to arise at unrelated times.

Instead, we are kept occupied by jobs that rarely allow for rest, bound by increasingly complex systems of laws, rules, and procedures that grow more intricate by the day. We are continuously reminded that advancing technology will simplify our lives, yet each passing day seems to prove the opposite. What if we were continuously being reminded to embrace our individual and collective powers, rather than to consider ourselves in need of synthetic enhancements?

It is true that we could disconnect, retreat to a rural setting, and sustain ourselves on food we grow or hunt. But doing so would mean stepping into obscurity, living in isolation - alone, separate from the collective. And singular individuals hold little power against the force of the collective.

Yet the collective remains distracted. Too busy to explore, identify, and harness the transformative spark within us all. Instead, we experience countless subtle clues. They come like tiny disturbances that invite us to shape our world differently, yet they go ignored, dismissed as we strive to keep pace with the endless demands placed upon us.

The second scarf dream, which occurred four years later, signalled that Kamala Harris represented the final opportunity to maintain the existing reality. As a woman of colour, she embodied a shift that only a US president from a similar background could fully achieve. Perhaps that shift was exactly what humanity needed - one that could ripple out from the US and become the next incarnation of a democratic society. Alternatively, her presidency might have preserved the status quo, leaving the world unchanged. We will never know which possibility might have come to pass because Kamala Harris did not become the US president.

Instead, Donald Trump ascended to the presidency. And remarkably, he aligns with the prophecy I first encountered in the 1980s, and that of Biblical Prophecy.

But what does that mean?

The French Dis-Connection clue

While Marine Le Pen may not directly align with the prophecy, she remains a significant figure in the geopolitical landscape. Born Marion Anne Perrine Le Pen, she is widely recognized as Marine Le Pen, leader of the far-right National Rally party. She ran for the French presidency in 2017 and 2022, advancing to the second round in both elections but ultimately losing to Emmanuel Macron.

In 2017, Le Pen positioned herself as a nationalist candidate, emphasizing opposition to the European Union and immigration. However, her campaign faced challenges, including lingering concerns about her party's historical ties to extremism and a poorly received debate performance against Macron. She secured around 35% of the vote, while Macron won with 65%.

At the time, Donald Trump was US President. After Le Pen praised his 2016 election victory, he expressed support for her, admiring her political resilience and hardline stance on immigration. Many saw this as further evidence of the growing momentum of nationalist movements worldwide.

In 2022, Le Pen sought to broaden her appeal by focusing on economic issues and attempting to distance herself from her party's more controversial past. While she increased her vote share compared to 2017, she was again defeated by Macron, who won with 58% of the vote. Her loss was attributed to concerns about her ties to Russia, scepticism regarding her economic policies, and Macron's ability to unite centrist and left-wing voters against her.

Despite her defeat, Le Pen's rising support reflected a notable shift in French politics, with the far-right gaining more mainstream appeal.

Following his return to office in 2025, President Trump publicly defended Le Pen after her conviction for embezzling EU funds, denouncing the case as a "witch hunt" and drawing comparisons to his own enduring legal battles.

While Le Pen does not fit the prophecy's criteria for an "unholy alliance" second world leader - primarily because she is female - her surname contains five letters, and she undeniably attracted the admiration and attention of the US President during both of her French presidential campaigns. Unlike Syria's Assad, Le Pen's name cannot be casually shortened to "Pen". Her transformational agenda for France would also have been directly counter to US democratic values, meeting the "unholy alliance" aspect of prophecy.

The recurring emergence of key individuals who bear striking resemblance to prophesied figures at precisely the right time and place raises an intriguing question: Could the apparent mismatches with certain prophecy criteria themselves be clues waiting to be deciphered?

The 3rd Temple Clue

The belief in the Third Temple is deeply rooted in biblical prophecy, with several groups anticipating its construction, each driven by distinct motivations. Within Jewish religious organizations, groups such as the Temple Institute actively prepare for its rebuilding, viewing it as a divinely ordained event that will usher in the Messianic era. Evangelical Christians, particularly those focused on eschatology, regard the Third Temple as a crucial step in the fulfillment of end-times prophecy, often linking it to the return of Christ. Some Messianic Jewish movements also embrace the belief that the temple is a key element of God's unfolding plan for Israel and humanity. Across these perspectives, the Third Temple represents hope, fulfillment, and the convergence of sacred destiny.

Yet is it possible that the Third Temple carries a meaning beyond traditional interpretations? Present-day understandings of the Temple's purpose are grounded in centuries-old interpretations—could its role have shifted? Could the very nature of the Temple itself have changed?

Consider the three branches of the U.S. government: the Executive, Legislative, and Judicial. What if these institutions function as symbolic "temples" that a modern figure exalts himself over? Suppose someone leads the Executive Branch while effectively nullifying the Legislative Branch through an excessive number of Executive Orders on trade policy, federal funding, and other financial matters that constitutionally fall under Congress's authority. Imagine further that this figure disregards a unanimous ruling by the Supreme Court. Could such actions be interpreted as a form of self-exaltation over three sacred pillars of U.S. democracy?

If these parallels hold significance, what might it reveal? Could it serve as a smaller-scale prelude to an antichrist event, offering an opportunity to test a Christ-consciousness response? Are we failing to recognize important prophetic moments unfolding before us?

The Nature of Time

Science has made remarkable progress in revealing that time is far more complex than the once-accepted notion of a simple, linear progression. While definitive proof that time is entirely non-linear remains elusive, scientific discoveries increasingly support the idea that time is multidimensional.

Einstein's theory of relativity, for example, fundamentally reshaped our understanding of time, demonstrating that it is not absolute but instead intricately woven into the four-dimensional fabric of spacetime. In this framework, time can appear to stretch or slow down depending on the observer's motion or gravitational influence. This means that time is not experienced identically by all observers; rather, events can occur in different sequences and durations depending on perspective - a direct challenge to the idea of time as singular, universal, or strictly linear.

Further interpretations of relativity suggest that past, present, and future may exist simultaneously. This concept, often referred to as the block universe or eternalism, proposes that time does not flow in the way human consciousness perceives it. Instead, it is a static dimension where events are laid out within a four-dimensional continuum.

Spacetime continuum theory suggests that the past is never truly lost, the future is already present, and our perception of moving through time may be more illusionary than a fundamental truth. Alongside this view, alternative theories such as presentism and quantum loop theory challenge linear interpretations of time, prompting questions about whether time truly progresses or if our experience of it is shaped by perception.

When considered in relation to prophecy, do these emerging theories on time, perception, and the eternal nature of past, present, and future indicate that foretelling the future may be, to some, a recording of the past or present to others? If so, who are these others? Is it possible that they are us - advanced beings who, through a deeper understanding of time, were able to record events as they unfolded, offering guidance or warnings for future generations?

Furthermore, if we were to reinterpret the entire Bible, analysing every word to ensure a literal translation within the current context of events, could this offer a roadmap for what comes next? Would such an approach unlock new insights into prophecy, enabling us to recognize patterns or instructions embedded within ancient texts?

Christ v Antichrist consciousness

There is another compelling reason to revisit the Bible and reinterpret it within the framework of today's scientific understanding. When the scriptures were originally written in Hebrew, Greek, and Aramaic, the scientific knowledge of the time was vastly different from what we know today. The perception of reality itself was shaped by ancient worldviews, influencing how concepts such as "light" and "darkness" were portrayed. Often, they were seen as interwoven yet opposing forces - symbols of good and evil, Christ and antichrist. But if we were to reexamine biblical texts in their original languages while integrating modern scientific insights, what might we uncover?

Einstein's renowned theory of relativity offers an intriguing perspective. His equation, $E=mc^2$, reveals that energy (E) and mass (m) are intricately connected, differentiated only by the speed of light squared (c^2). Could this formula serve as a key to understanding Christ Consciousness?

Is it possible that Christ Consciousness represents energy, the missing light factor which is absent in mass? And when mass and light combine, does it form an energy that transcends the physical realm into something spiritual? Could Einstein's discovery of the relationships between energy, mass, and light speed reflect the deeper connection between the material and spiritual worlds?

Biblical prophecy foretells that the antichrist will emerge toward the end of the age, performing significant actions and ushering in transformative events - until the return of Christ. But if the return of Christ signifies the resurgence of Christ Consciousness - the energy Einstein described - and the awakening of the spiritual realm, then prophecy may not simply be predicting inevitable events, but rather issuing a call to action. If Christ is within each of us, as scripture suggests, then are we meant to respond to prophecy rather than passively witness it unfold?

The events and correlations that I have kept record of, and which appear to bear an uncanny resemblance to prophecy, seem to evidence a repeated effort to send Humanity a message. Is it possible that the message is an invitation, continuously repeated until we finally acknowledge it? Could prophecy exist not to warn humanity of an unchangeable future but to empower us to shape it? Rather than leaving us powerless and reactionary, does prophecy challenge us to design the world we wish to live in?

If each of us carries the essence of Christ, then we already possess the power to overcome. We must embrace the belief that we are whole, capable, and perfectly equipped to manifest the reality we collectively envision. However, to do so, we must shift our focus. Instead of dwelling on the forces of the antichrist - mass devoid of light - we must elevate our energy, our spirit, and drive a quantum transformation into a new state of existence.

Building our New World

How does humanity evolve its approach to prophecy if its true purpose is to inspire action? What if prophecy is not simply a warning but a call to engage - an invitation to awaken and channel our collective Christ Consciousness? How do we shift from apocalyptic anxiety, consumed by fear of an unknown future, to hope, empowerment, and unified purpose?

The first step is to recognize the deeper truth: we are focusing on darkness without acknowledging the light that is interwoven within it - the same light that resides within each of us. We must understand that our challenge is not merely a battle against corrupt individuals, misguided policies, or authoritarian geopolitics. The real obstacle is our own reductionist thinking, our tendency to interpret prophecy in a linear fashion rather than recognizing the multidimensional nature of our existence. We stand within a spacetime phenomenon where past, present, and future are far more intertwined than traditional religious or scientific models can adequately define.

Moving forward demands that we counter bleak narratives with a more expansive vision of survival - one that embraces interconnection, ensuring that no single aspect of existence is left behind. We must rewrite the script that fuels the gothic appeal of end-times fatalism and instead ignite a movement rooted in collective resilience. This is not a tale of inevitable collapse but a summons for transformation. It is not a path of isolation and dominance, but one that elevates interdependence and belonging. It calls us to remain anchored in the realities of our world, not lost in fantasies of a distant Zion or waiting for intervention.

This perspective is neither new nor radical. It echoes Indigenous cosmologies and ancient animist principles that venerate the present rather than an imagined future. Perhaps, when prophecy appears to be unfolding, it is less about an unavoidable destiny and more about a moment of choice - an opportunity to shape the trajectory of reality through our decisions.

Perhaps our greatest mistake is thinking of ourselves as disconnected individuals, trapped by disagreement and unable to act. Maybe the solution isn't found in mapping every step before acting, but rather in joining together first, trusting that clarity and direction will emerge once unity is achieved.

If we commit to the present as though it holds the same weight as both past and future, could we shift our perspective away from fear and destruction? Could we instead, steer humanity toward a future of possibility, beauty, and joy?

I am often reminded of the following quote by pioneering environmentalist and conservationist, David Brower, which is painted as a welcome sign on an indigenous campsite, not far from my home:

> *"We don't inherit the earth from our ancestors; we borrow it from our children."*

It is time to break free from the weight of our past and recognize that prophecy is not merely a forecast of fate. It is a collection of clues guiding us toward a future we have the power to create. No longer confined by what once was, we must embrace the wisdom embedded in prophetic insights, not as warnings to fear, but as instructions for building something greater. The future is not a predetermined path but a landscape of unfolding possibilities, shaped by the choices we make.

Prophecy does not dictate an inevitable fate; rather, it offers a framework to help us recognize our options and navigate the way forward. Instead of being bound by the past, we must step fully into our ability to shape what comes next, using prophecy as a tool for clarity and action rather than limitation. The future is a dynamic canvas, waiting for us to decide how we bring it to life.

Acknowledgements

To the watchers, the listeners, the thinkers, and the seekers—this book is, in many ways, yours as much as it is mine.

To those who have joined me in conversation. Who have followed my work across social media, who have tuned in to the radio waves, who have shared, subscribed, and carried my voice further than I could have reached alone - you are the foundation on which these words rest. Your support, whether through engagement, donations, or simply the act of showing up with curiosity, has shaped this journey.

To those who have read my previous work, who have invested in these ideas, who have encouraged me with messages of inspiration, personal stories, and quiet understanding—you remind me that I am never alone in asking the questions that matter.

And to those unseen but present - the ones who observe from the shadows, who recognize the importance of a voice searching through the haze, who understand that I am not the answer but the questioner seeking truth - your awareness means everything. You know that truth does not reside in rigid certainty but in the space between, in the willingness to explore the unknown.

To the ordinary, the average, the everyday individuals across the world - regardless of language, nationality, or belief system - who sense that there is more than what we are led to believe, who hold open minds to the possibility that answers may arrive in unexpected ways... this book is for you.

For every person who has ever wondered, who has ever questioned, who has ever felt the pull toward something beyond the surface:

Thank you. Your search is what keeps the conversation alive.

Sources and Further Reading

Australia:

Aboriginal and Torres Strait Islander Voice. Indigenous.gov.au. Available at: https://www.indigenous.gov.au/aboriginal-and-torres-strait-islander-voice

Australia Life Expectancy 1950-2025. Macrotrends. Available at: https://www.macrotrends.net/global-metrics/countries/AUS/australia/life-expectancy

International Comparisons of Welfare Data. Australian Institute of Health and Welfare. Available at: https://www.aihw.gov.au/reports/australias-welfare/international-comparisons-of-welfare-data

Life Expectancy. Australian Bureau of Statistics. Available at: https://www.abs.gov.au/statistics/people/population/life-expectancy/latest-release

What is the Implied Right to Freedom of Political Communication in Australia? NSW Courts. Available at: https://nswcourts.com.au/articles/what-is-the-implied-right-to-freedom-of-political-communication-in-australia/

Canada:

Canada Life Expectancy 1950-2025. Macrotrends. Available at: https://www.macrotrends.net/global-metrics/countries/CAN/canada/life-expectancy

Canadian Charter of Rights and Freedoms. Justice Canada. Available at: https://www.justice.gc.ca/eng/csj-sjc/rfc-dlc/ccrf-ccdl/

Healthcare for Real: How Does Canada Rank in Healthcare? Canadian Medical Association. Available at: https://www.cma.ca/healthcare-for-real/how-does-canada-rank-health-care

Life Expectancy in Canada: Recent Trends. Statistics Canada. Available at: https://wWorld War One50.statcan.gc.ca/n1/daily-quotidien/250305/dq250305a-eng.htm

The Guide to the Canadian Charter of Rights and Freedoms. Canada.ca. Available at: https://www.canada.ca/en/canadian-heritage/services/how-rights-protected/guide-canadian-charter-rights-freedoms.html

Germany:

Basic Law for the Federal Republic of Germany. Wikipedia. Available at: https://en.wikipedia.org/wiki/Basic_Law_for_the_Federal_Republic_of_Germany

Deaths, Life Expectancy. Destatis (German Federal Statistical Office). Available at: https://www.destatis.de/EN/Themes/Society-Environment/Population/Deaths-Life-Expectancy/_node.html

Germany Life Expectancy 1950-2025. Macrotrends. Available at: https://www.macrotrends.net/global-metrics/countries/DEU/germany/life-expectancy

Germany - Health and Welfare. Encyclopaedia Britannica. Available at: https://www.britannica.com/place/Germany/Health-and-welfare

United Kingdom:

Human Rights Act 1998. Legislation.gov.uk. Available at: https://www.legislation.gov.uk/ukpga/1998/42/contents

National Life Tables: United Kingdom, 2020-2022. Office for National Statistics. Available at: https://www.ons.gov.uk/peoplepopulationandcommunity/birthsdeat

hsandmarriages/lifeexpectancies/bulletins/nationallifetablesunitedkingdom/2020to2022

United Kingdom Life Expectancy 1950-2025. Macrotrends. Available at: https://www.macrotrends.net/global-metrics/countries/GBR/united-kingdom/life-expectancy

United Kingdom: Social Policies. Sustainable Governance Indicators. Available at: https://www.sgi-network.org/2019/United_Kingdom/Social_Policies

UK Parliament Research Briefing. (2022). Commonwealth Bill of Rights? (CBP-9819). House of Commons Library. Retrieved from https://researchbriefings.files.parliament.uk/documents/CBP-9819/CBP-9819.pdf

United States:

Bush v. Gore, 531 U.S. 98 (2000).

Constitution of the United States. Congress.gov. Available at: https://constitution.congress.gov/constitution/amendment-1/

FastStats - Life Expectancy. Centers for Disease Control and Prevention. Available at: https://www.cdc.gov/nchs/fastats/life-expectancy.htm

First Amendment to the United States Constitution. Wikipedia. Available at: https://en.wikipedia.org/wiki/First_Amendment_to_the_United_States_Constitution

New International Study: U.S. Health System Ranks Last Among 11 Countries; Many Americans Struggle to Afford Care as Income Inequality Widens. Commonwealth Fund. Available at: https://www.commonwealthfund.org/press-release/2021/new-international-study-us-health-system-ranks-last-among-11-countries-many

United States Life Expectancy 1950-2025. Macrotrends. Available at: https://www.macrotrends.net/global-metrics/countries/USA/united-states/life-expectancy

News and Politics:

Freedom in the World 2025: Uphill Battle to Safeguard Rights. Freedom House. Available at: https://freedomhouse.org/report/freedom-world/2025/uphill-battle-to-safeguard-rights

ABC News. (2023, August 25). China, Russia, BRICS expansion: Iran, Saudi Arabia, Xi, Putin. Australian Broadcasting Corporation. https://www.abc.net.au/news/2023-08-25/china-russia-brics-expansion-iran-saudi-arabia-xi-putin/102774406

Al Jazeera. (2024, September 18). Hezbollah and Israel: A timeline of conflict. Al Jazeera. Retrieved from https://www.aljazeera.com/news/2024/9/18/hezbollah-and-israel-a-timeline-of-conflict

Barlow, K. (2025, April 12). We are being tested: Inside Labor's trade war strategy. The Saturday Paper. https://www.thesaturdaypaper.com.au/news/politics/2025/04/12/we-are-being-tested-inside-labors-trade-war-strategy

Burns, M. (2025, April 16). Memo to Washington insiders: Stop pretending that Trump is normal! Common Dreams. https://www.commondreams.org/opinion/stop-pretending-trump-normal

CBS News. (2018, July 16). Trump sides with Putin over U.S. intelligence in remarkable Helsinki press conference. Retrieved from https://www.cbsnews.com/news/trump-sides-with-putin-over-u-s-intelligence-in-remarkable-helsinki-press-conference/

Daily News Hungary. (2025, March 5). Orbán-Trump phone call. Retrieved from https://dailynewshungary.com/orban-trump-phone-call/

Doe, J. (2025, January 15). Trump and the disruption of the policy status quo. Baker Institute.
https://www.bakerinstitute.org/research/trump-and-disruption-policy-status-quo

Harvard Gazette. (2025, March). Where next for the U.S. economy? Retrieved from
https://news.harvard.edu/gazette/story/2025/03/where-next-for-the-u-s-economy/

Harvard Law School. (2022, February 17). When Nixon went to China. Retrieved from https://hls.harvard.edu/today/when-nixon-went-to-china/

Harvey, S. (2025, February 5). What Donald Trump said on Gaza — his statement in full. The Independent. Retrieved from
https://www.independent.co.uk/news/world/americas/us-politics/donald-trump-gaza-statement-full-b2692486.html

Inside Political Science. (n.d.). Gridlock in Congress: Examples. Retrieved from https://insidepoliticalscience.com/gridlock-in-congress-examples/

Jamal, U. (2023, August 25). Analysis: What do BRICS invitations mean for the Middle East? Al Jazeera.
https://www.aljazeera.com/news/2023/8/25/analysis-what-do-brics-invitations-mean-for-the-middle-east

Jenkins, B. M. (2023, March 7). Consequences of the war in Ukraine: The economic fallout. RAND Corporation.
https://www.rand.org/pubs/commentary/2023/03/consequences-of-the-war-in-ukraine-the-economic-fallout.html

Jones, S. (2017, March 3). Vladimir Putin asked Bill Clinton about Russia joining NATO. The Guardian. Retrieved from
https://www.theguardian.com/world/2017/mar/03/vladimir-putin-asked-bill-clinton-about-russia-joining-nato

Kelley, Alexandra. "US ranks last in worker benefits among developed countries: data." The Hill, February 4, 2021. Available at:

https://thehill.com/changing-america/respect/equality/537359-us-ranks-last-in-worker-benefits-among-developed-countries/

Klien, N. Taylor, A. The Guardian. (2025, April 13). End times fascism: Far right, Trump, Musk. https://www.theguardian.com/us-news/ng-interactive/2025/apr/13/end-times-fascism-far-right-trump-musk

Newsweek. (2024, November 6). Viktor Orbán and Donald Trump: President plans. Retrieved from https://www.newsweek.com/viktor-orban-donald-trump-president-plans-1981770

Panetta, A. (2025, March 18). U.S. could lose democracy status, says global watchdog. CBC News. Retrieved from https://www.cbc.ca/news/world/trump-democracy-report-1.7486317

Pen Agency News. (2024, November 22). Russia-Ukraine war: NATO's role and the international impact. https://www.penagencynews.com/russia-ukraine-war-natos-role-and-the-international-impact/

Phillips, Amber. (2020, March 6). Who are the women probably on Joe Biden's shortlist for vice president? Washington Post. https://www.washingtonpost.com/politics/2020/03/15/which-woman-would-biden-pick-vice-president/

Retirely. (2025). From bad to worse: 15 ugly U.S. cities facing continued decline. Retrieved from https://retirely.co/from-bad-to-worse-15-ugly-u-s-cities-facing-continued-decline/

Reuters. (2025, April 7). Ukraine aims to align with US on minerals deal in talks this week. Reuters. https://www.reuters.com/world/ukraine-aims-align-with-us-minerals-deal-talks-this-week-2025-04-07/

Robles, C. (2025, April 14). El Salvador's president says he won't return deported man held in high-security prison. BNO News. https://bnonews.com/index.php/2025/04/el-salvadors-president-says-he-wont-return-deported-man-held-in-high-security-prison/

Scheiring, G. (2024, March 7). I watched Hungary's democracy dissolve into authoritarianism as a member of parliament – and I see troubling parallels in Trumpism and its appeal to workers. The Conversation. Retrieved from https://theconversation.com/i-watched-hungarys-democracy-dissolve-into-authoritarianism-as-a-member-of-parliament-and-i-see-troubling-parallels-in-trumpism-and-its-appeal-to-workers-224930

The Straits Times. (2018, July 11). Donald Trump and Theresa May: Six key moments in their 'special relationship'. Retrieved from https://www.straitstimes.com/world/europe/donald-trump-and-theresa-may-six-key-moments-in-their-special-relationship

Timelines:

10 reasons for the collapse of the Soviet Union. WorldAtlas (nd). Retrieved from https://www.worldatlas.com/articles/10-reasons-for-the-collapse-of-the-soviet-union.html

Decline of the British Empire. Encyclopedia Britannica(nd). Retrieved from https://www.britannica.com/summary/Decline-of-the-British-Empire

Why did the Soviet Union collapse? Encyclopaedia Britannica (nd). Retrieved from https://www.britannica.com/story/why-did-the-soviet-union-collapse

Abbott, Daniel (2010). The Handbook of Fifth-Generation Warfare. Nimble Books.

Acemoglu, D., & Robinson, J. A. (2012). WHY NATIONS FAIL: THE ORIGINS OF POWER, PROSPERITY, AND POVERTY. Crown Business.

History Hit. (n.d.). Ukraine and Russia: The history post-USSR. Retrieved from https://www.historyhit.com/ukraine-and-russia-history-post-ussr/

Holy Bible. (1982). New King James Version. Thomas Nelson.

Matthew 24:3. The Holy Bible. (2011). New International Version. Zondervan. (Original work published 1978).

Renaissance timeline. Encyclopedia Britannica (nd). Retrieved from https://www.britannica.com/summary/Renaissance-Timeline

The Enlightenment: Causes and effects. Encyclopedia Britannica. Retrieved from https://www.britannica.com/summary/The-Enlightenment-Causes-and-Effects

The Holy Bible. (1769/2017). King James Version. Cambridge University Press. (Original work published 1611).

Western philosophy. Encyclopaedia Britannica. (nd). Retrieved from https://www.britannica.com/topic/Western-philosophy

Human Context:

60 Minutes Australia. (2025, May 4). Why people are falling in love with A.I. companions [Television broadcast]. Nine Network.

Boyer, P. (2005). Give me that end-time religion: The politicization of prophetic belief in contemporary America. Reflections. Yale Divinity School. Retrieved from https://reflections.yale.edu/article/end-times-and-end-gamesis-scripture-being-left-behind/give-me-end-time-religion

Braden, G. (2025). Pure human: The hidden truth of our divinity, power, and destiny (Hardcover ed.). Hay House LLC.

Consciousness in the Age of Artificial Intelligence. Transpersonal Psychology (2025). Retrieved from https://transpersonal-psychology.iresearchnet.com/technology-virtual-reality-and-consciousness/consciousness-in-the-age-of-artificial-intelligence/

Democracy Index 2020. Economist Intelligence Unit. (2020). Available at: https://www.eiu.com/n/campaigns/democracy-index-2020/

Freedom in the World 2021. Freedom House. (2021). Available at: https://freedomhouse.org/report/freedom-world/2021/democracy-under-siege

Freud, S. (1913). Totem and Taboo: Resemblances between the psychic lives of savages and neurotics. Moffat, Yard and Company.

Nietzsche, F. (1887). On the Genealogy of Morals: A Polemic. C. G. Naumann.

Public trust in government: 1958-2024. Pew Research Center. (2024, June 24). Available at: https://www.pewresearch.org/politics/2024/06/24/public-trust-in-government-1958-2024/

Seong, J., White, O., Birshan, M., Smit, S., Lamanna, C., & Devesa, T. (2025, January). Geopolitics and the geometry of global trade: 2025 update.

Maslow, A. H. (1954). Motivation and personality. Harpers

McKinsey Global Institute. https://www.mckinsey.com/mgi/our-research/geopolitics-and-the-geometry-of-global-trade-2025-update

Consumers take fright at U.S. policy trajectory and other key economic news to know. World Economic Forum. (2025, March). Retrieved from https://www.weforum.org/stories/2025/03/consumers-take-fright-at-us-policy-trajectory-and-other-key-economic-news-to-know/

> Why empires and civilizations collapse: A look at the factors leading to societal collapse. (2024, April 26). The Archaeologist. https://www.thearchaeologist.org/blog/why-empires-and-civilizations-collapse-a-look-at-the-factors-leading-to-societal-collapse

World Press Freedom Index 2024. Reporters Without Borders. Available at: https://rsf.org/en/index

Tate, K. (2022). Normalizing Abuse: A Commentary on the Culture of Pervasive Abuse. Karen Tate.

Other:

Baba Vanga 2020 prediction: Did the blind mystic warn of coronavirus? Express. (2020, March 16).Retrieved from https://www.express.co.uk/news/weird/1256073/Baba-Vanga-2020-prediction-coronavirus-blind-mystic-COVID19-virus-prophecy

Institute of Biomedical Science. (2018). The management of laboratory training

JFK was killed over UAP transparency desire: intelligence officer. (2025, March 23). Reality check with Ross Coulthart [Video]. NewsNation. YouTube. https://www.youtube.com/watch?v=mHzVOXCnakY&list=PL6PrA6lo8rJLRExhMvX6wKyNzyohr_QM3&index=12

Magnificent 7 - The glorious seven shares - Everything you need to know. Captrader. (2025, March 29). Retrieved April 11, 2025, from https://www.captrader.com/en/blog/magnificent-seven-the-glorious-seven-shares-everything-you-need-to-know/

What is the Age of Conscious-Technology? World Economic Forum. (2015). Retrieved from https://www.weforum.org/stories/2015/01/what-is-the-age-of-conscious-technology/

What is Magnificent 7? The history of the Big Tech abbreviation behind it. EWC. (nd). Information. Retrieved April 11, 2025, from https://www.ewc.co.jp/en/information/3981/

www.ingramcontent.com/pod-product-compliance
Lightning Source LLC
Chambersburg PA
CBHW051855160426
43209CB00006B/1313